C

C

Missouri
BIRDS

Michael Roedel
Gregory Kennedy

LONE
PINE

Lone Pine Publishing International

The Distributor: Lone Pine Publishing
1808 B Street NW, Suite 140
Auburn, WA, USA 98001

Website: www.lonepinepublishing.com

Library and Archives Canada Cataloguing in Publication

Roedel, Michael, 1955-
    Compact guide to Missouri birds / Michael Roedel, Gregory Kennedy.

Includes bibliographical references and index.
ISBN-13: 978-976-8200-02-0
ISBN-10: 976-8200-02-2

    1. Birds--Missouri--Identification. 2. Bird watching--Missouri.
I. Kennedy, Gregory, 1956- II. Title.

QL684.M8R63 2006   598'.0978   C2005-907612-7

Cover Illustration: Wood Duck by Gary Ross
Illustrations: Gary Ross, Ted Nordhagen, Eva Pluciennik
Separations & Film: Elite Lithographers Co.
Egg Photography: Allan Bibby, Gary Whyte

We would like to thank the Royal Alberta Museum for giving us access to their egg collection.

PC: 13

Contents

WATERFOWL

Canada Goose
size 42 in • p. 18

Wood Duck
size 17 in • p. 20

Mallard
size 24 in • p. 22

Common Goldeneye
size 18 in • p. 24

Common Merganser
size 24 in • p. 26

Wild Turkey
size 40 in • p. 28

TURKEYS & QUAILS

Northern Bobwhite
size 10 in • p. 30

Great Blue Heron
size 52 in • p. 32

Cattle Egret
size 20 in • p. 34

HERONS & VULTURES

Green Heron
size 18 in • p. 36

Turkey Vulture
size 28 in • p. 38

Bald Eagle
size 36 in • p. 40

BIRDS OF PREY

Broad-winged Hawk
size 16 in • p. 42

Red-tailed Hawk
size 21 in • p. 44

American Kestrel
size 8 in • p. 46

COOTS

SHOREBIRDS

American Coot
size 14 in • p. 48

American Golden-Plover
size 10 in • p. 50

Killdeer
size 10 in • p. 52

Lesser Yellowlegs
size 10 in • p. 54

Pectoral Sandpiper
size 9 in • p. 56

Wilson's Snipe
size 11 in • p. 58

Franklin's Gull
size 14 in • p. 60

Ring-billed Gull
size 19 in • p. 62

Forster's Tern
size 15 in • p. 64

Rock Pigeon
size 12 in • p. 66

Mourning Dove
size 12 in • p. 68

Yellow-billed Cuckoo
size 12 in • p. 70

Eastern Screech-Owl
size 8 in • p. 72

Great Horned Owl
size 22 in • p. 74

Barred Owl
size 20 in • p. 76

Common Nighthawk
size 9 in • p. 78

Whip-poor-will
size 9 in • p. 80

Chimney Swift
size 5 in • p. 82

Ruby-throated Hummingbird
size 4 in • p. 84

Belted Kingfisher
size 12 in • p. 86

Red-headed Woodpecker
size 9 in • p. 88

SHOREBIRDS

GULLS & TERNS

DOVES & CUCKOOS

OWLS

NIGHTJARS
& HUMMINGBIRDS

WOODPECKERS

WOODPECKERS

Red-bellied Woodpecker
size 10 in • p. 90

Downy Woodpecker
size 6 in • p. 92

Northern Flicker
size 12 in • p. 94

FLYCATCHERS

Pileated Woodpecker
size 16 in • p. 96

Eastern Wood-Pewee
size 6 in • p. 98

Acadian Flycatcher
size 6 in • p. 100

Eastern Phoebe
size 7 in • p. 102

Great Crested Flycatcher
size 8 in • p. 104

Eastern Kingbird
size 9 in • p. 106

VIREOS

JAYS & CROWS

Red-eyed Vireo
size 6 in • p. 108

Blue Jay
size 11 in • p. 110

American Crow
size 18 in • p. 112

LARKS & SWALLOWS

Horned Lark
size 7 in • p. 114

Purple Martin
size 8 in • p. 116

Northern Rough-winged Swallow
size 5 in • p. 118

CHICKADEES, WRENS & NUTHATCHES

Barn Swallow
size 7 in • p. 120

Carolina Chickadee
size 4 in • p. 122

Tufted Titmouse
size 6 in • p. 124

CHICKADEES, WRENS & NUTHATCHES

White-breasted Nuthatch
size 6 in • p. 126

Carolina Wren
size 5 in • p. 128

Eastern Bluebird
size 7 in • p. 130

THRUSHES

Wood Thrush
size 8 in • p. 132

American Robin
size 10 in • p. 134

Gray Catbird
size 9 in • p. 136

MIMICS, STARLINGS & WAXWINGS

Northern Mockingbird
size 10 in • p. 138

Brown Thrasher
size 11 in • p. 140

European Starling
size 8 in • p. 142

Cedar Waxwing
size 7 in • p. 144

Northern Parula
size 5 in • p. 146

American Redstart
size 5 in • p. 148

WOOD-WARBLERS & TANAGERS

Louisiana Waterthrush
size 6 in • p. 150

Common Yellowthroat
size 5 in • p. 152

Yellow-breasted Chat
size 7 in • p. 154

Summer Tanager
size 7 in • p. 156

Eastern Towhee
size 8 in • p. 158

Field Sparrow
size 5 in • p. 160

SPARROWS & GROSBEAKS

SPARROWS & GROSBEAKS

Dark-eyed Junco
size 6 in • p. 162

Northern Cardinal
size 8 in • p. 164

Rose-breasted Grosbeak
size 8 in • p. 166

Blue Grosbeak
size 7 in • p. 168

Indigo Bunting
size 5 in • p. 170

Red-winged Blackbird
size 8 in • p. 172

BLACKBIRDS & ALLIES

Eastern Meadowlark
size 9 in • p. 174

Brown-headed Cowbird
size 7 in • p. 176

Orchard Oriole
size 7 in • p. 178

FINCHLIKE BIRDS

American Goldfinch
size 5 in • p. 180

House Sparrow
size 6 in • p. 182

Introduction

If you have ever admired a songbird's pleasant notes, been fascinated by a soaring hawk or wondered how woodpeckers keep sawdust out of their nostrils, this book is for you. There is so much to discover about birds and their surroundings that birding is becoming one of the fastest growing hobbies on the planet. Many people find it relaxing, while others enjoy its outdoor appeal. Some people see it as a way to reconnect with nature, an opportunity to socialize with like-minded people or a way to monitor the environment.

Whether you are just beginning to take an interest in birds or can already identify many species, there is always more to learn. We've highlighted both the remarkable traits and the more typical behaviors displayed by some of our most abundant or noteworthy birds. A few live in specialized habitats, but most are common species that you have a good chance of encountering on most outings or in your backyard.

Pileated Woodpecker

BIRDING IN THE WOODLANDS

We are truly blessed by the geographical and biological diversity of Missouri. In addition to supporting a wide range of breeding birds and year-round residents, our state hosts a large number of spring and fall migrants that move through our area on the way to their breeding and wintering grounds. In all, more than 400 bird species have been seen and recorded in Missouri.

Identifying birds in action and under varying conditions involves skill, timing and luck. The more you know about a bird—its range, preferred habitat, food preferences, and hours and seasons of activity—the better your chances will be of seeing it. Generally, spring and fall are the busiest birding times. Temperatures are moderate then, many species of birds are on the move, and male songbirds are belting out their unique courtship songs. Birds are usually most active in the early morning hours, except in winter, when they forage during the day when milder temperatures prevail.

Another useful clue for correctly recognizing birds is knowledge of their habitat. Simply put, a bird's habitat is the place where it normally lives. Some birds prefer open water, some are found in cattail marshes, others like mature coniferous forests, and still others prefer abandoned agricultural fields overgrown with tall grass and shrubs. Habitats are just like neighborhoods: if you associate friends with the suburb in which they live, you can easily learn to associate specific birds with their preferred habitat. Only in migration, especially during inclement weather, do some birds leave their usual habitat.

American Redstart

Missouri has a long tradition of friendly, recreational birding. In general, birders are willing to help beginners, share their knowledge and involve novices in their projects. Christmas bird counts, breeding bird surveys, nest box programs, migration monitoring, and birding lectures and workshops provide a chance for bird-watchers of all levels to interact and share the splendor of birds. Bird hotlines provide up-to-date information

Barred Owl

on the sightings of rarities, which are often easier to relocate than you might think. For more information or to partici-pate in these projects, contact the following organizations:

Audubon Society of Missouri
2101 West Broadway #122, Columbia, MO 65203
http://mobirds.org/

Missouri Department of Conservation
http://mdc.mo.gov/

BIRD LISTING

Many birders list the species they have seen during excur-sions or at home. It is up to you to decide what kind of list—systematic or casual—you will keep, and you may choose not to make lists at all. Lists may prove rewarding in unexpected ways, and after you visit a new area, your list becomes a souvenir of your experiences there. Keeping regular, accurate lists of birds in your neighborhood can also be useful for local researchers. It can be interesting to compare the arrival dates and last sightings of humming-birds and other seasonal visitors, or to note the first sight-ing of a new visitor to your area.

BIRD FEEDING

Many people set up bird feeders in their backyard, especially in winter. It is possi-ble to attract specific birds by choosing the right kind of food and style of feeder. Keep your feeder stocked through late spring, because birds have a hard time find-ing food before the flowers bloom, seeds develop and insects hatch. Contrary to popular opinion, birds do not become dependent on

Cedar Waxwing

feeders, nor do they subsequently forget to forage naturally. Be sure to clean your feeder and the surrounding area regularly to prevent the spread of disease.

Landscaping your property with native plants is another way of providing natural food for birds. Flocks of waxwings have a keen eye for red mountain ash berries and hummingbirds enjoy columbine flowers. The cumulative effects of "nature-scaping" urban yards can be a significant step toward habitat conservation (especially when you consider that habitat is often lost in small amounts—a seismic line is cut in one area and a highway is built in another). Many good books and web sites about attracting wildlife to your backyard are available.

Common Yellowthroat

NEST BOXES

Another popular way to attract birds is to put up nest boxes, especially for House Wrens, Eastern Bluebirds, Tree Swallows and Purple Martins. Not all birds will use nest boxes; only species that normally use cavities in trees are comfortable in such confined spaces. Larger nest boxes can attract kestrels, owls and cavity-nesting ducks.

White-breasted Nuthatch

ABOUT THE SPECIES ACCOUNTS

Chimney Swift

This book gives detailed accounts of 83 species of birds that can be expected in Missouri on an annual basis. The order of the birds and their common and scientific names follow the American Ornithologists' Union's *Check-list of North American Birds* (7th edition, July 1998, and its supplements through 2005).

As well as showing the identifying features of the bird, each species account also attempts to bring the bird to life by describing its various character traits. One of the challenges of birding is that many species look different in spring and summer than they do in fall and winter. Many birds have breeding and nonbreeding plumages, and immature birds often look different from their parents. This book does not try to describe or illustrate all the different plumages of a species; instead, it tries to focus on the forms that are most likely to be seen in our area.

ID: Large illustrations point out prominent field marks that will help you tell each bird apart. The descriptions favor easily understood language instead of technical terms.

Other ID: This section lists additional identifying features. Some of the most common anatomical features of birds are pointed out in the Glossary illustration (p. 185).

Size: The average length of the bird's body from bill to tail, as well as wingspan, are given and are approximate measurements of the bird as it is seen in nature. The size is sometimes given as a range, because there is variation between individuals, or between males and females.

Voice: You will hear many birds, particularly songbirds, which may remain hidden from view. Memorable paraphrases of distinctive sounds will aid you in identifying a species by ear.

Status: A general comment, such as "common," "uncommon" or "rare," is usually sufficient to describe the relative abundance of a species. Situations are bound to vary somewhat since migratory pulses, seasonal changes and centers of activity tend to concentrate or disperse birds.

Habitat: The habitats listed describe where each species is most commonly found. Because of the freedom that flight gives them, birds can turn up in almost any type of habitat.

Orchard Oriole

However, they will usually be found in environments that provide the specific food, water, cover and, in some cases, nesting habitat that they need to survive.

Similar Birds: Easily confused species are illustrated for each account. If you concentrate on the most relevant field marks, the subtle differences between species can be reduced to easily identifiable traits. Even experienced birders can mistake one species for another.

Nesting: In each species account, nest location and structure, clutch size, incubation period and parental duties are discussed. A photo of the bird's egg is also provided. Remember that birding ethics discourage the disturbance of active bird nests. If you disturb a nest, you may drive off the parents during a critical period or expose defenseless young to predators.

Red-bellied Woodpecker

Range Maps: The range map for each species shows the overall range of the species in an average year. Most birds will confine their annual movements to this range, though each year some birds wander beyond their traditional boundaries. The maps show breeding, summer and winter ranges, as well as migratory pathways—areas of the region where birds may appear while en route to nesting or winter habitat. The representations of the pathways do not distinguish high-use migration corridors from areas that are seldom used.

Dark-eyed Junco

Range Map Symbols

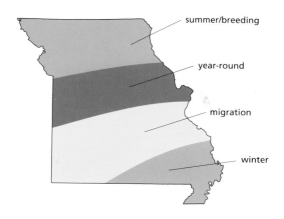

summer/breeding

year-round

migration

winter

TOP BIRDING SITES

From the lowlands of the Mississippi Floodplain to the breathtaking Ozarks, our state can be separated into four natural regions: the Central Tallgrass Prairie, the Osage Plains–Flint Hills Prairie, the Ozarks and the Mississippi River Alluvial Plain. Each region is composed of a number of different habitats that support a wealth of wildlife.

There are hundreds of good birding areas throughout our region. The following areas have been selected to represent a broad range of bird communities and habitats, with an emphasis on accessibility.

1. Squaw Creek NWR
2. Swan Lake NWR
3. Ted Shanks Conservation Area
4. Eagle Bluffs Conservation Area
5. Riverlands Environmental Demonstration Area
6. August A. Busch Memorial Conservation Area
7. Taberville Prairie
8. Hercules Glades Wilderness
9. Ozark National Scenic Riverways
10. Mingo NWR
11. Lake of the Ozarks SP
12. Big Oak Tree SP
13. Dexter rice fields
14. Cuivre River SP
15. Fleming Park
16. Smithville Reservoir
17. Prairie SP
18. Springville area
19. Roaring River SP

NWR National Wildlife Refuge
SP State Park

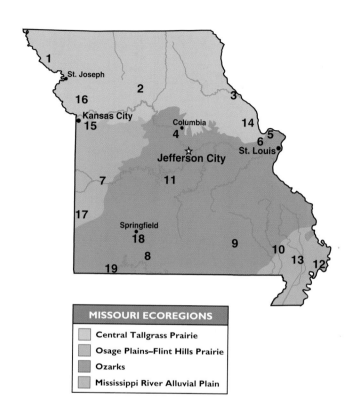

MISSOURI ECOREGIONS

	Central Tallgrass Prairie
	Osage Plains–Flint Hills Prairie
	Ozarks
	Mississippi River Alluvial Plain

St. Joseph

Kansas City

Columbia

Jefferson City

St. Louis

Springfield

1
2
3
16
15
14
5
6
4
7
11
17
18
8
9
10
13
12
19

Canada Goose
Branta canadensis

Thousands of Canada Geese once descended on Missouri each winter, but these large flocks now overwinter farther north. Many cut short their migration to enjoy the abundant food supply found in the corn and grain fields that cover the Midwest. Although some migratory geese regularly visit Missouri each year, there are now many more resident nonmigratory individuals and flocks. • The Canada Goose was split into two species in 2004. The larger subspecies continue to be known as the Canada Goose, but the smaller subspecies were reclassified as the Cackling Goose. • Currently, wild Canada Geese breed along the bluffs of the Missouri River; all other breeding geese have been reintroduced from captive stock.

Other ID: dark brown upperparts; light brown underparts. *In flight:* flocks fly in V-formation.
Size: *L* 3–4 ft; *W* up to 6 ft.
Voice: loud, familiar *ah-honk*.
Status: common permanent resident.
Habitat: lakeshores, riverbanks, ponds, farmlands and city parks.

Similar Birds

Cackling Goose

Brant

Greater White-fronted Goose

long, black neck

white "chin strap"

short, black tail

white undertail coverts

Nesting: usually on the ground; female builds a nest of grass and mud lined with down; white eggs are 3½ x 2¼ in; female incubates 3–8 eggs for 25–28 days; goslings hatch in May.

Did You Know?

Canada Geese mate for life, but unlike most young birds, goslings remain with their devoted parents for nearly a year.

Look For

Geese graze on aquatic grasses and sprouts, and you can spot them tipping up to grab for aquatic roots and tubers.

Wood Duck

Aix sponsa

A forest-dwelling duck, the Wood Duck is equipped with claws for perching on branches and nesting in tree cavities. • Shortly after hatching, the ducklings jump out of their nest cavity, often falling 20 feet or more. Like downy ping-pong balls, they bounce on landing and are seldom injured. • Female Wood Ducks often return to the same nest site year after year, especially after successfully raising a brood. Established nest sites, where the adults are familiar with potential threats, may improve the chance of survival for the young.

Other ID: *Male:* glossy, green head with some white streaks; white-spotted, purplish chestnut breast; black-and-white shoulder slash; dark back and hindquarters. *Female:* gray-brown upperparts; white belly.
Size: *L* 15–20 in; *W* 30 in.
Voice: *Male:* ascending *ter-wee-wee*. *Female:* squeaky *woo-e-e-k*.
Status: common migrant and summer resident; uncommon winter resident.
Habitat: swamps, ponds, marshes and lakeshores with wooded edges.

Similar Birds

Hooded Merganser

Look For

A male Wood Duck defending his mate from other suitors will often strike the interloper with an open wing when he gets too close.

head raised in flight ♂

♀

white "teardrop" eye patch

golden sides

crest slicked back from crown

♀

♂

white "chin" and throat

mottled brown breast streaked with white

Nesting: in a hollow, tree cavity or artificial nest box; usually near water; cavity is lined with down; white to buff eggs are 2⅛ x 1⅝ in; female incubates 9–14 eggs for 25–35 days.

Did You Know?

Landowners with a small, treelined pond or other suitable wetland may attract a family of Wood Ducks by building a suitably sized nest box with a predator guard and lining it with sawdust. The nest box should be close to the shoreline and at least 5 feet from the ground.

Mallard
Anas platyrhynchos

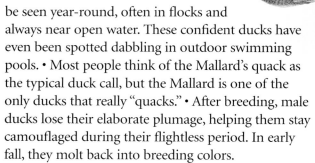

The male Mallard, with his shiny, green head and chestnut brown breast, is the classic wild duck. Mallards can be seen year-round, often in flocks and always near open water. These confident ducks have even been spotted dabbling in outdoor swimming pools. • Most people think of the Mallard's quack as the typical duck call, but the Mallard is one of the only ducks that really "quacks." • After breeding, male ducks lose their elaborate plumage, helping them stay camouflaged during their flightless period. In early fall, they molt back into breeding colors.

Other ID: orange feet. *Male:* white "necklace"; black tail feathers curl upward. *Female:* mottled brown overall.
Size: L 20–28 in; W 3 ft.
Voice: quacks; female is louder than male.
Status: common permanent resident; most abundant during migration.
Habitat: lakes, wetlands, rivers, city parks, agricultural areas and sewage lagoons.

Similar Birds

Northern Shoveler

American Black Duck

Common Merganser
(p. 26)

glossy, green head

yellow bill

dark blue speculum
bordered by white

orange bill spattered
with black

♂   ♀

Nesting: a grass nest is built on the ground or
under a bush; creamy, grayish or greenish white
eggs are 2¼ x 1⅝ in; female incubates 7–10 eggs
for 26–30 days.

Did You Know?

A nesting hen generates
enough body heat to make
the grasses around her
nest grow faster. She uses
the tall grasses to further
conceal her precious nest.

Look For

Mallards readily hybridize
with a variety of other duck
species, including common
barnyard ducks, often producing offspring with very
peculiar plumages.

Common Goldeneye
Bucephala clangula

The typical Common Goldeneye spends its entire life in North America, dividing its time between breeding grounds in the boreal forests of Canada and Alaska and its winter territory in marine bays and estuaries along the Atlantic and Pacific coasts. The largest numbers are seen along the Mississippi River in late February or early March, but this bird is also common on large rivers and lakes throughout winter. • Fish, crustaceans and mollusks make up a major portion of the Common Goldeneye's winter diet, but in summer, this diving duck eats a lot of aquatic invertebrates and tubers.

Other ID: golden eyes. *Male:* iridescent, dark green head; dark back; white sides and belly. *Female:* lighter breast and belly; gray-brown body plumage; yellow tip on dark bill in spring and summer.
Size: *L* 16–20 in; *W* 26 in.
Voice: generally silent in migration and winter. *Male:* nasal *peent* and hoarse *kraaagh* in courtship. *Female:* harsh croak.
Status: common winter resident.
Habitat: open water of lakes, reservoirs, large ponds and rivers.

Similar Birds

Bufflehead

Hooded Merganser

black wings with large, white patches ♂

♀

chocolate brown head

dark bill

steep forehead with peaked crown

white, oval "cheek" patch ♂

♀

Nesting: does not nest in Missouri; nests mainly in Canada; in a tree cavity or occasionally a nest box lined with wood chips and down; often close to water; blue-green eggs are 2⅜ x 1⅝ in; female incubates 6–10 eggs for 28–32 days.

Did You Know?

In winter, female Common Goldeneyes fly farther south than males, and immature birds continue even farther south.

Look For

Common Goldeneyes are frequently called "Whistlers," because the wind whistles through their wings when they fly.

Common Merganser
Mergus merganser

Lumbering like a jumbo jet, the Common Merganser must run along the surface of the water, beating its heavy wings to gain sufficient lift to take off. Once up and away, this large duck flies arrow-straight and low over the water, making broad, sweeping turns to follow the meandering shorelines of rivers and lakes. • Common Mergansers are highly social and often gather in large groups during migration. In winter, any source of open water with a fish-filled shoal will support good numbers of these skilled divers.

Other ID: large, elongated body. *Male:* white body plumage; black stripe on back; dark eyes. *Female:* gray body; orangy eyes. *In flight:* shallow wingbeats; body is compressed and arrowlike.
Size: L 22–27 in; W 34 in.
Voice: *Male:* harsh *uig-a*, like a guitar twang. *Female:* harsh *karr karr*.
Status: fairly common winter resident.
Habitat: large rivers and deep lakes.

Similar Birds

Red-breasted Merganser

Northern Shoveler

Common Loon

glossy, green head
without crest

rusty neck and
crested head

blood red bill
and feet

orange bill

clean white "chin"
and breast

Nesting: does not nest in Missouri; nests in
Canada and western U.S.; in a tree cavity;
occasionally on the ground or in a large nest box;
usually close to water; pale buff eggs are 2½ x
1¾ in; female incubates 8–11 eggs for 30–35 days.

Did You Know?

The Common Merganser
is the most widespread
and abundant merganser
in North America. It also
occurs in Europe and Asia.

Look For

In flight, the Common
Merganser has shallow
wingbeats and an arrowlike,
compressed body.

Wild Turkey
Meleagris gallopavo

The Wild Turkey was once very common through-out most of eastern North America, but during the early 20th century, habitat loss and overhunting took a toll on this bird. Today, efforts at restoration have reestablished the Wild Turkey statewide. • This charismatic bird is the only native North American animal that has been widely domesticated. The wild ancestors of most other domestic animals came from Europe. • Early in life, both male and female turkeys gobble. The females eventually outgrow this practice, leaving males to gobble competitively for the honor of mating.

Other ID: largely unfeathered legs. *Male:* red wattles, black-tipped breast feathers. *Female:* smaller; blue-gray head; less iridescent body; brown-tipped breast feathers.
Size: *Male: L* 3–3½ ft; *W* 5½ ft. *Female: L* 3 ft; *W* 4 ft.
Voice: courting male gobbles loudly; alarm call is a loud *pert;* gathering call is a cluck; contact call is a loud *keouk-keouk-keouk.*
Status: common permanent resident.
Habitat: deciduous, mixed and riparian wood-lands with clearings; occasionally eats waste grain and corn in late fall and winter.

Look For

Eastern Wild Turkeys have brown or rusty tail tips and are slimmer than domestic turkeys, which have white tail tips. Turkeys prefer to feed on the ground and travel by foot (they can run faster than 19 miles per hour), but they are able to fly short distances, and they roost in trees at night.

naked, blue-red head

dark, glossy, iridescent body plumage

barred, copper-colored tail

♂

long central breast tassel

Nesting: under thick cover in a woodland or at a field edge; in a depression on ground, lined with vegetation; brown-speckled, pale buff eggs are 2½ x 1¾ in; female incubates 10–12 eggs for up to 28 days.

Did You Know?

If Congress had taken Benjamin Franklin's advice in 1782, our national emblem would be the Wild Turkey instead of the majestic Bald Eagle.

Northern Bobwhite
Colinus virginianus

The characteristic whistled *bob-white* call of our only native quail is heard throughout Missouri in spring. The male's well-known call is often the only evidence of this bird's presence among the dense, tangled vegetation of its rural, woodland home.
• In fall and winter, Northern Bobwhite typically travel in large family groups called coveys. When a predator approaches, the covey bursts into flight, creating a confusing flurry of activity. With the arrival of summer, breeding pairs break away from their coveys to perform elaborate courtship rituals in preparation for another nesting season.

Other ID: mottled brown, buff and black upperparts; white crescents and spots edged in black on chestnut brown sides and upper breast; short tail.
Size: L 10 in; W 13 in.
Voice: whistled *hoy* is given year-round. *Male:* whistled, rising *bob-white* in spring and summer.
Status: common permanent resident.
Habitat: farmlands, open woodlands, woodland edges, grassy fencelines, roadside ditches and brushy, open country.

Similar Birds

Ruffed Grouse

Greater Prairie-Chicken

broad, white "eyebrow"

buff throat and "eyebrow"

white throat

♂

♀

Nesting: in a shallow depression on the ground, often concealed by vegetation or a woven, partial dome; nest is lined with grass and leaves; white to pale buff eggs are 1¼ x 1 in; pair incubates 12–16 eggs for 22–24 days.

Did You Know?

Bobwhite huddle together on cold winter nights, with each bird facing outward, enabling the group to detect danger from any direction.

Look For

Bobwhite benefit from habitat disturbance and are often found in the early succession habitats created by fire, agriculture and forestry.

Great Blue Heron
Ardea herodias

The long-legged Great Blue Heron is the tallest of all North American herons. It has a stealthy, often motionless hunting strategy. The heron waits for a fish or frog to approach, spears the prey with its bill, then flips its catch into the air and swallows the prey whole. Herons usually hunt near water, but they also stalk fields and meadows in search of rodents. • Great Blue Herons settle in communal treetop nesting sites called rookeries. Most nesting colonies are found in southern Missouri. Nesting herons are sensitive to human disturbance, so observe this bird's behavior from a distance.

Other ID: blue-gray overall; long, dark legs. *Breeding:* richer colors; plumes streak from crown and throat. *In flight:* black upperwing tips; legs trail behind body; slow, steady wingbeats.
Size: L 4¼–4½ ft; W 6 ft.
Voice: quiet away from the nest; occasional harsh *frahnk frahnk frahnk* during takeoff.
Status: common summer resident; uncommon winter resident.
Habitat: forages along edges of rivers, lakes and marshes; also in fields and wet meadows.

Similar Birds

Little Blue Heron

Look For

In flight, the Great Blue Heron folds its neck back over its shoulders in an S-shape. Similar-looking cranes stretch their necks out when flying.

neck folds back over shoulders

black plumes

dark crown

straight, yellow bill

breeding

long, curving neck with black markings on throat

chestnut brown thighs

Nesting: colonial; adds to stick platform nest over years; nest width can reach 4 ft; pale bluish green eggs are 2½ x 1¾ in; pair incubates 4–7 eggs for about 28 days.

Did You Know?

Fossil records show that the Great Blue Heron has been present in North America since 1.8 million years ago, around the time when mammoths and saber-toothed cats also roamed our continent.

Cattle Egret
Bubulcus ibis

In the agricultural fields of the Mississippi Lowlands, stoic groups of Cattle Egrets stare silently as people rush past in speeding vehicles. Over the last century—and without help from humans—the Cattle Egret has dispersed from Africa to inhabit pastureland and roadsides on every continent except Antarctica. These natural wanderers spread from Africa to Brazil, then, by the 1940s, to Florida and across the United States. • Cattle Egrets follow tractors or grazing animals, catching any insects that are stirred up. Invertebrates make up a main portion of their diet, unlike other egrets, which eat mainly fish.

Other ID: *Breeding:* long plumes on throat and rump; purple lores. *Nonbreeding:* yellow-orange bill; black legs.
Size: L 19–21 in; W 35–37 in.
Voice: generally silent away from breeding colony; most common call is an unmusical *rick-rack*.
Status: fairly common migrant and local summer resident.
Habitat: agricultural fields, ranchlands and marshes.

Similar Birds

Great Egret

Snowy Egret

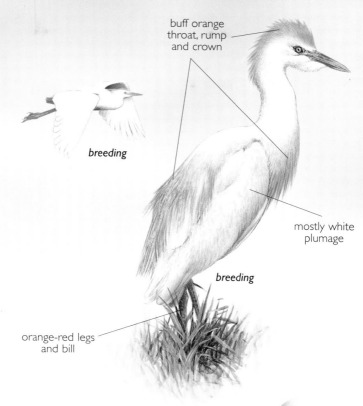

buff orange throat, rump and crown

breeding

mostly white plumage

breeding

orange-red legs and bill

Nesting: colonial; often among other herons; in a tree or tall shrub; male supplies sticks for female, who builds a platform or shallow bowl; pale blue eggs are 1¾ x 1⅜ in; pair incubates 3–4 eggs for 21–26 days.

Did You Know?

This bird's scientific name *Bubulcus* means "belonging to or concerning cattle."

Look For

When foraging, the Cattle Egret sometimes uses a "leapfrog" feeding strategy, in which birds leap over one another, stirring up insects for the birds that follow.

Green Heron
Butorides virescens

Sentinel of mangroves and marshes, the ever-vigilant Green Heron sits hunched on a shaded branch at the water's edge. This crow-sized heron stalks frogs and small fish lurking in the weedy shallows, then stabs prey with its sturdy bill. • Unlike most herons, the Green Heron nests singly rather than communally, though it can sometimes be found in loose colonies. Although some of this heron's habitat has been lost to wetland drainage or channelization in the southern states, the building of farm ponds or reservoirs has created habitat in other areas.

Other ID: stocky body; relatively short, yellow-green legs; long bill is dark above and greenish below; short tail. *Breeding male:* bright orange legs.
Size: L 15–22 in; W 26 in.
Voice: generally silent; alarm and flight call are a loud *kowp, kyow* or *skow*; aggression call is a harsh *raah*.
Status: common summer resident.
Habitat: marshes, lakes and streams with dense shoreline or emergent vegetation, mangroves.

Similar Birds

Black-crowned
Night-Heron

Least Bittern

American Bittern

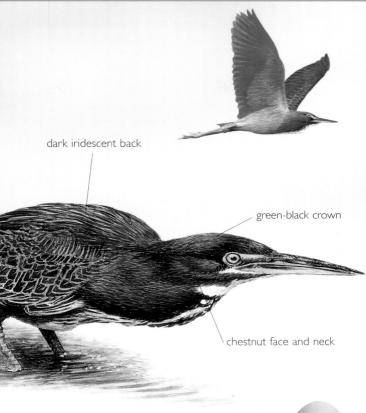

dark iridescent back

green-black crown

chestnut face and neck

Nesting: nests singly or in small, loose groups; stick platform in a tree or shrub, usually close to water; blue-green to green eggs are 1½ x 1⅛ in; pair incubates 3–5 eggs for 19–21 days.

Did You Know?

Green Herons have been seen baiting fish to the surface by dropping small bits of debris such as twigs, vegetation or feathers.

Look For

The scientific name *virescens* is Latin for "growing or becoming green" and refers to this bird's transition from a streaky brown juvenile to a greenish adult.

Turkey Vulture

Cathartes aura

Turkey Vultures are intelligent, playful and social birds. Groups live and sleep together in large trees, or "roosts." Some roost sites are over a century old and have been used by the same family of vultures for several generations. • The scientific name *Cathartes* means "cleanser" and refers to this bird's affinity for carrion. A vulture's bill and feet are much less powerful than those of eagles, hawks or falcons, which kill live prey. Its red, featherless head may appear grotesque, but this adaptation allows the bird to stay relatively clean while feeding on messy carcasses.

Other ID: *Immature:* gray head. *In flight:* head appears small; rocks from side to side when soaring.
Size: *L* 25–31 in; *W* 5½–6 ft.
Voice: generally silent; occasionally produces a hiss or grunt if threatened.
Status: common summer resident; uncommon winter resident.
Habitat: usually flies over open country, shorelines or roads; rarely over forests.

Similar Birds

Black Vulture

Golden Eagle

Bald Eagle (p. 40)

silver gray flight feathers

holds wings in a shallow "V"

bare, red head

pale, hooked bill

brownsih black overall

Nesting: in a cave, crevice, log or among boulders; uses little or no nest material; dull white eggs, irregularly marked with brown or purple, are 2¾ x 2 in; pair incubates 2 eggs for up to 41 days.

Did You Know?

A threatened Turkey Vulture may play dead or throw up. The odor of its vomit repulses attackers, much like the odor of a skunk's spray.

Look For

No other bird uses updrafts and thermals in flight as well as the Turkey Vulture. Pilots have reported seeing vultures soaring at 20,000 feet.

Bald Eagle
Haliaeetus leucocephalus

This majestic sea eagle hunts mostly fish and is often found near water. While soaring hundreds of feet high in the air, an eagle can spot fish swimming underwater and small rodents scurrying through the grass. Bald Eagles also scavenge carrion and steal food from other birds. • Bald Eagles do not mature until their fourth or fifth year—only then will they develop the characteristic white head and tail plumage.

immature

Other ID: *1st-year:* dark overall; dark bill; some white in underwings. *2nd-year:* dark "bib"; white in underwings. *3rd-year:* mostly white plumage; yellow at base of bill; yellow eyes. *4th-year:* light head with dark facial streak; variable pale and dark plumage; yellow bill; paler eyes.
Size: *L* 30–43 in; *W* 5½–8 ft.
Voice: thin, weak squeal or gull-like cackle: *kleek-kik-kik-kik* or *kah-kah-kah.*
Status: uncommon migrant and summer resident; increasingly common winter resident; remains federally threatened.
Habitat: large lakes and rivers.

Similar Birds

Golden Eagle

Osprey

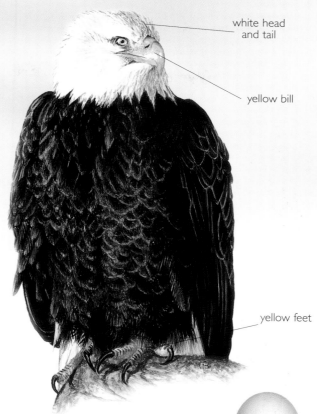

white head
and tail

yellow bill

yellow feet

Nesting: in a tree; usually, but not always, near water; huge stick nest is often reused for many years; white eggs are 2¾ x 2⅛ in; pair incubates 1–3 eggs for 34–36 days.

Did You Know?

The Bald Eagle, a symbol of freedom, longevity and strength, became the emblem of the United States in 1782.

Look For

Bald Eagles mate for life and renew pair bonds by adding sticks to their nests, which can be up to 15 feet in diameter, the largest of any North American bird.

Broad-winged Hawk
Buteo platypterus

light morph

The best time to see Broad-winged Hawks in Missouri is during fall migration, when "kettles" of these buteos migrate south to wintering grounds in Central and South America. Hundreds or sometimes thousands of these hawks take advantage of warm, thermal air currents to soar, sometimes gliding for hours without flapping. • This shy hawk prefers dense, often wet forests. In this habitat, its short, broad wings and highly flexible tail help it to maneuver in the heavy growth.

Other ID: broad wings with pointed tips; dark brown upperparts. *Dark morph:* rare; dark brown overall; dark underwing coverts in flight.
Size: *L* 14–19 in; *W* 32–39 in.
Voice: high-pitched, whistled *peeeo-wee-ee;* generally silent during migration.
Status: fairly common migrant; uncommon summer resident in southern Missouri.
Habitat: *Breeding:* dense, mixed and deciduous forests and woodlots. *In migration:* escarpments and shorelines; also riparian and deciduous forests and woodland edges.

Similar Birds

Red-shouldered Hawk

Red-tailed Hawk (p. 44)

dark "mustache" stripe

heavily barred, rufous brown breast

broad black and white tail bands

pale underwings outlined with dark brown

light morph

Nesting: usually in a deciduous tree; often near water; bulky stick nest; usually builds a new nest each year; brown-spotted, whitish eggs are 2 x 1½ in; female incubates 2–4 eggs for 28–31 days; both adults raise the young.

Did You Know?

Of all the raptors, the Broad-winged Hawk is the most likely to be seen clutching a snake.

Look For

This hawk likes to hunt from a high perch with a good view. If flushed from its perch, the Broad-winged Hawk will soon return and resume its vigilant search for a meal.

Red-tailed Hawk
Buteo jamaicensis

Take an afternoon drive through the country and look for Red-tailed Hawks soaring above the fields. Red-tails are the most common hawks in Missouri, especially in winter. • In warm weather, these hawks use thermals and updrafts to soar. The pockets of rising air provide substantial lift, which allows migrating hawks to fly for almost 2 miles without flapping their wings. On cooler days, resident Red-tails perch on exposed tree limbs, fence posts or utility poles to scan for prey.

Other ID: brown eyes; overall color varies geographically. *In flight:* light underwing flight feathers with faint barring; dark leading edge on underside of wing.
Size: *Male: L* 18–23 in; W 4–5 ft. *Female:* L 20–25 in; W 4–5 ft.
Voice: powerful, descending scream: *keeearrrr.*
Status: common permanent resident.
Habitat: open country with some trees; also roadsides or woodlots.

Similar Birds

Broad-winged Hawk
(p. 42)

Red-shouldered Hawk

Swainson's Hawk

dark "shoulder" patches

dark upperparts with some white highlights

dark brown band of streaks across belly

red tail

Nesting: in woodlands adjacent to open habitat; bulky stick nest is enlarged each year; brown-blotched, whitish eggs are 2⅜ x 1⅞ in; pair incubates 2–4 eggs for 28–35 days.

Did You Know?

The Red-tailed Hawk's piercing call is often paired with the image of an eagle in TV commercials and movies.

Look For

Courting Red-tails will sometimes dive at one another, lock talons and tumble toward the earth, breaking away at the last second to avoid crashing into the ground.

American Kestrel
Falco sparverius

The colorful American Kestrel, formerly known as the "Sparrow Hawk," is a common and widespread falcon, not shy of human activity and adaptable to habitat change. This small falcon has benefited from the grassy right-of-ways created by interstate highways, which provide habitat for grasshoppers and other small prey. Watch for this robin-sized bird along rural roadways, perched on poles and telephone wires or hovering over agricultural fields, foraging for insects and small mammals. • The American Kestrel's diminutive size allows it to nest in tree cavities; these excellent locations help protect defenseless young kestrels from hungry predators.

Other ID: lightly spotted underparts. *In flight:* frequently hovers; buoyant, indirect flight style.
Size: L 7½–8 in; W 20–24 in.
Voice: usually silent; loud, often repeated, shrill *killy-killy-killy* when excited; female's voice is lower pitched.
Status: common permanent resident.
Habitat: open fields, riparian woodlands, wood-lots, forest edges, bogs, roadside ditches, grassy highway medians, grasslands and croplands.

Similar Birds

Merlin

Peregrine Falcon

Sharp-shinned Hawk

2 distinctive
facial stripes

blue-gray
crown with
rusty cap

long, rusty
tail

rusty barring
on back

♀

rusty wings
and breast
streaking

♂

blue-gray wings

Nesting: in a tree cavity; may use a nest box; white to pale brown, spotted eggs are 1½ x 1⅛ in; mostly the female incubates 4–6 eggs for 29–30 days; both adults raise the young.

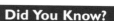

Did You Know?

No stranger to captivity, the American Kestrel was the first falcon to reproduce by artificial insemination.

Look For

An American Kestrel will repeatedly lift its tail while perched as it scouts below for prey.

American Coot
Fulica americana

American Coots resemble ducks but are more closely related to rails and gallinules. The number of coots that breed here fluctuates yearly but good numbers regularly appear on our lakes, reservoirs and wetlands from late September to May. During winter these birds are aggressive and territorial, running along the surface of the water and charging intruders. A confrontational coot will stab with its bill while trying to grab the perpetrator with one clawed foot. • With feet that have individually webbed toes, the coot is adapted to diving, but it isn't afraid to snatch a meal from another diver when a succulent piece of water celery is brought to the surface.

Other ID: red eyes; long, yellow-green legs; lobed toes.
Size: *L* 13–16 in; *W* 24 in.
Voice: calls frequently in summer, day and night: *kuk-kuk-kuk-kuk-kuk;* also croaks and grunts.
Status: common in migration and winter; rare in summer.
Habitat: shallow marshes, ponds and wetlands with open water and emergent vegetation; also sewage lagoons.

Similar Birds

Pied-billed Grebe

Purple Gallinule

Common Moorhen

reddish spot on white forehead shield

white, chicken-like bill with dark ring around tip

small white marks on tail

gray-black overall

Nesting: in emergent vegetation; pair builds float-ing nest of cattails and grass; buffy white, brown-spotted eggs are 2 x 1⅜ in; pair incubates 8–12 eggs for 21–25 days; may raise 2 broods.

Did You Know?

American Coots are the most widespread and abundant members of the rail family in North America.

Look For

Though it somewhat resem-bles a duck, an American Coot bobs its head while swimming or walking and has a narrower bill that extends up the forehead.

American Golden-Plover

Pluvialis dominica

A mere 150 years ago, the American Golden-Plover population was among the largest of any bird in the world, but in the late 1800s, market gunners mercilessly culled the great flocks—a single day's shooting often yielded tens of thousands of birds. Populations have recovered somewhat, but will likely never return to their former numbers.

• Missouri birders get a chance to see the American Golden-Plover's striking breeding plumage from late March to mid-May, as large flocks migrate through, en route to the Arctic.

Other ID: straight, black bill; long, black legs. *Breeding:* black face and underparts; upperparts speckled with gold and white. *Nonbreeding:* broad, pale "eyebrow"; dark streaking on pale neck and underparts; much less gold on upperparts.
Size: *L* 10–11 in; *W* 26 in.
Voice: flight call is a soft, melodious whistle: *quee, quee-dle.*
Status: fairly common in migration.
Habitat: cultivated fields, especially soybeans and corn; meadows; airports; also lakeshores and mudflats along the edges of reservoirs, marshes or sewage lagoons.

Similar Birds

Black-bellied Plover

Look For

The white stripe down this plover's side disrupts the vision of a predator, confusing the hunter as to where the bird's head or tail is.

gray "wing pits"

white stripe from
forehead down to
shoulders

dark cap

nonbreeding

black
undertail
coverts

♀

♂

breeding

Nesting: does not nest in Missouri; nests in the
Arctic; on the ground in dry tundra in a shallow
depression lined with grass, leaves, moss and
lichen; heavily marked, creamy buff eggs are 2 x 1⅝
in; pair incubates 4 eggs for 26–27 days.

Did You Know?

The cryptic coloration of speckles on this bird's upperparts
blends well with the golden, mottled earth of its arctic
breeding grounds. Although the bird is boldly marked, the
pattern breaks up the image of the bird on the tundra.

Killdeer

Charadrius vociferus

The Killdeer is a gifted actor, well known for its "broken wing" distraction display. When an intruder wanders too close to its nest, the Killdeer greets the interloper with piteous cries while dragging a wing and stumbling about as if injured. Most predators take the bait and follow, and once the Killdeer has lured the predator far away from its nest, it miraculously recovers from the injury and flies off with a loud call.

Other ID: brown head; white neck band; brown back and upperwings; white underparts; rufous rump. *Immature:* downy; only 1 breast band.
Size: *L* 9–11 in; *W* 24 in.
Voice: loud, distinctive *kill-dee kill-dee kill-deer;* variations include *deer-deer.*
Status: common permanent resident.
Habitat: open areas, such as fields, lakeshores, sandy beaches, mudflats, gravel streambeds, wet meadows and grasslands.

Similar Birds

Semipalmated Plover   Piping Plover

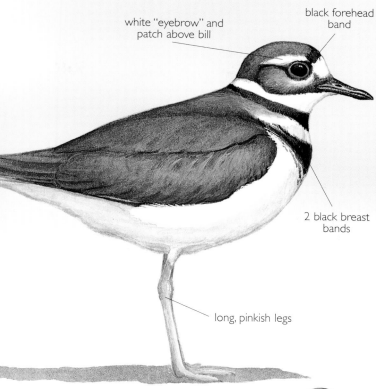

white "eyebrow" and patch above bill

black forehead band

2 black breast bands

long, pinkish legs

Nesting: on open ground, in a shallow, usually unlined depression; heavily marked, creamy buff eggs are 1⅜ x 1⅛ in; pair incubates 4 eggs for 24–28 days; may raise 2 broods.

Did You Know?

In spring, you might hear a European Starling imitate the vocal Killdeer's call.

Look For

The Killdeer has adapted well to urbanization, and it can be seen on golf courses, farms, fields and in abandoned industrial areas as often as on shorelines.

Lesser Yellowlegs
Tringa flavipes

The "tattletale" Lesser Yellowlegs is the self-appointed sentinel in a mixed flock of shorebirds, raising the alarm at the first sign of a threat. • It is challenging to discern Lesser Yellowlegs and Greater Yellowlegs (*T. melanoleuca*) in the field, but with practice, you will notice that the Lesser's bill is finer, straighter and shorter—about as long as its head is wide. With long legs and wings, the Lesser appears slimmer and taller than the Greater, and it is more commonly seen in flocks. Finally, the Lesser Yellowlegs emits a pair of peeps, but the Greater Yellowlegs peeps three times.

Other ID: subtle, dark eye line; pale lores. *Nonbreeding:* grayer overall.
Size: L 10–11 in; W 24 in.
Voice: typically a high-pitched pair of *tew* notes; noisiest on breeding grounds.
Status: common migrant.
Habitat: shorelines of lakes, rivers, marshes and ponds; coastal mudflats.

Similar Birds

Willet

Greater Yellowlegs

Solitary Sandpiper

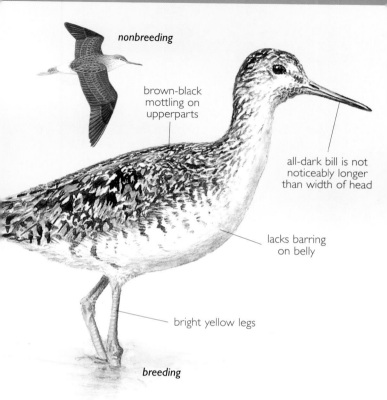

nonbreeding

brown-black
mottling on
upperparts

all-dark bill is not
noticeably longer
than width of head

lacks barring
on belly

bright yellow legs

breeding

Nesting: does not nest in Missouri; nests in the Arctic; in open muskeg or a natural forest opening; in a depression on a dry mound lined with leaves and grass; darkly blotched, buff to olive eggs are 1⅝ x 1⅛ in; pair incubates 4 eggs for 22–23 days.

Did You Know?

Yellowlegs were popular game birds in the 1800s because they were plentiful and easy to shoot.

Look For

When feeding, the Lesser Yellowlegs wades into water almost to its belly, sweeping its bill back and forth just below the water's surface.

Pectoral Sandpiper
Calidris melanotos

Pectoral Sandpipers get their name from the location of the male's prominent air sacs. When displaying on its arctic breeding grounds, the male will inflate these air sacs, causing his breast feathers to rise. Males also emit a hollow hooting sound during displays that has been likened to the sound of a foghorn. • This widespread traveler has been observed in every state and province in North America during its epic annual migrations. In spring and fall, large flocks of hundreds or even thousands of Pectoral Sandpipers are conspicuous in wet, grassy fields and along shorelines.

Other ID: white undertail coverts; black bill has slightly downcurved tip; mottled upperparts; may have faintly rusty, dark crown and back; folded wings extend beyond tail. *Immature:* less spotting on breast; broader white feather edges on back form 2 white "V"s.
Size: *L* 9 in; *W* 18 in (female is noticeably smaller).
Voice: sharp, short, low *krrick krrick*.
Status: common in migration.
Habitat: lakeshores, marshes, mudflats and flooded fields or pastures.

Similar Birds

White-rumped
Sandpiper

Semipalmated
Sandpiper

Least Sandpiper

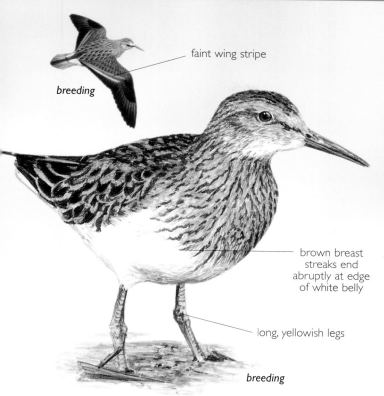

faint wing stripe

breeding

brown breast streaks end abruptly at edge of white belly

long, yellowish legs

breeding

Nesting: does not nest in Missouri; nests in the Arctic; on flat, wet tundra with grass-sedge cover; in a shallow depression lined with grass; brown-blotched, pale olive eggs are 1½ x 1 in; female incubates 4 eggs for 21–23 days.

Did You Know?

Pectoral Sandpipers are sometimes referred to as "Grass Snipes" because of their preference for wet meadows and grassy marshes.

Look For

Unlike most sandpipers, the Pectoral exhibits sexual dimorphism—the female is only two-thirds the size of the male.

Wilson's Snipe
Gallinago delicata

When flushed from cover, snipes perform a series of aerial zigzags to confuse predators. Because of this habit, hunters who were skilled enough to shoot snipes became known as "snipers," a term later adopted by the military. • Courting snipes make an eerie, winnowing sound, like a rapidly hooting owl. The male's specialized outer tail feathers vibrate rapidly in the air as he performs daring, headfirst dives high above a wetland. Wilson's Snipes breed from Iowa northward, where they can be heard displaying day and night in spring.

Other ID: unmarked, white belly; relatively short legs. *In flight:* quick zigzags on takeoff.
Size: L 10½–11½ in; W 18 in.
Voice: in flight, courtship song is an eerie, accelerating *woo-woo-woo-woo-woo-woo;* often sings *wheat wheat wheat* from an elevated perch; alarm call is a nasal *scaip.*
Status: common in migration.
Habitat: cattail and bulrush marshes, sedge meadows, poorly drained floodplains, bogs and fens; willow and red-osier dogwood tangles.

Similar Birds

Short-billed Dowitcher

Long-billed Dowitcher

American Woodcock

heavily striped head, back and neck

dark eye stripe

rusty orange tail

long, sturdy, bicolored bill

dark barring on breast and flanks

Nesting: does not breed in Missouri; breeds from central U.S. northward; usually in dry grass; nest is made of grass, moss and leaves; darkly marked, olive buff to brown eggs are 1½ x 1⅛ in; female incubates 4 eggs for 18–20 days.

Did You Know?

The snipe's eyes are placed far back on its head, allowing it to see both forward and backward.

Look For

A snipe often plunges its entire head underwater while probing the shallows for tasty aquatic critters.

Franklin's Gull
Larus pipixcan

The Franklin's Gull is not a typical "sea gull." This land-loving bird spends much of its life inland and nests on the prairies, where it is affectionately known as "Prairie Dove." It often follows tractors across agricultural fields, snatching up insects from the tractor's path in much the same way its cousins follow fishing boats. • Franklin's Gull is one of only two gull species that migrate long distances between breeding and wintering grounds—the majority of Franklin's Gulls overwinter along the Pacific Coast of Peru and Chile.

Other ID: gray mantle; white underparts. *Breeding:* black head; red-orange bill and legs; breast often has pinkish tinge.

Size: *L* 13–15 in; *W* 3 ft.

Voice: shrill, "mewing" *weeeh-ah weeeh-ah* while feeding and in migration; also a shrill *kuk-kuk-kuk.*

Status: common in migration.

Habitat: agricultural fields, marshy lakes, landfills and large river and lake shorelines.

Similar Birds

Bonaparte's Gull

Laughing Gull

Common Tern

black crescent on white wing tips

incomplete, white eye ring

dark patch on back of white head

nonbreeding

black legs

nonbreeding

Nesting: does not nest in Missouri; nests in the Canadian prairies and northern Great Plains; colonial; usually in dense emergent vegetation; floating platform nest is built above water; variably marked, pale greenish or buff eggs are 2 x 1⅜ in; pair incubates 3 eggs for 25 days.

Did You Know?

This gull was named for Sir John Franklin, the British navigator and explorer who led four expeditions to the Canadian Arctic in the 19th century.

Look For

Large flocks of these gulls may linger on Missouri's lakes and large rivers during fall migration. In spring, smaller flocks move through the breeding grounds more quickly.

Ring-billed Gull

Larus delawarensis

Few people can claim that they have never seen this common and widespread gull. Highly tolerant of humans, Ring-billed Gulls are part of our everyday lives, scavenging our litter and fouling our parks. These omnivorous gulls will eat almost anything, and they will swarm parks, beaches, golf courses and fast-food restaurant parking lots looking for food handouts, making pests of themselves. However, few species have adjusted to human development as well as the Ring-billed Gull, which is something to appreciate.

Other ID: white head and underparts. *In flight:* black wing tips with a few white spots.
Size: *L* 18–20 in; *W* 4 ft.
Voice: high-pitched *kakakaka-akakaka;* also a low, laughlike *yook-yook-yook.*
Status: common winter resident in southern Missouri.
Habitat: lakes, rivers, landfills, golf courses, fields and parks.

Similar Birds

Herring Gull

Glaucous Gull

Thayer's Gull

nonbreeding

yellow eyes

pale gray mantle

black ring
around bill tip

yellow bill
and legs

nonbreeding

Nesting: does not nest in Missouri; breeds in northern U.S. and Canada; colonial; in a shallow scrape on the ground lined with grass, debris and small sticks; brown-blotched, gray to olive eggs are $2\frac{3}{8}$ x $1\frac{5}{8}$ in; pair incubates 2–4 eggs for 23–28 days.

Did You Know?

In chaotic nesting colonies, adult Ring-billed Gulls will call out and can recognize the response of their chicks.

Look For

To differentiate between gulls, pay attention to the markings on their bills and the color of their legs and eyes.

Forster's Tern
Sterna forsteri

The Forster's Tern so closely resembles the Common Tern *(S. hirundo)* that the two often seem indistinguishable to the eyes of many observers. Only when these terns acquire their distinctive fall plumages do birders begin to note the Forster's presence.

• Forster's Tern has an exclusively North American breeding distribution, but it bears the name of a man who never visited this continent: German naturalist Johann Reinhold Forster (1729–98). Forster, who lived and worked in England, examined tern specimens sent from Hudson Bay, Canada. He was the first to recognize this bird as a distinct species.

Other ID: *Breeding:* light gray mantle; white rump. *Nonbreeding:* black band through eyes; black bill. *In flight:* forked, gray tail; long, pointed wings.
Size: *L* 14–16 in; *W* 31 in.
Voice: flight call is a nasal, short *keer keer;* also a grating *tzaap.*
Status: common in migration.
Habitat: coastal areas; brackish wetlands; freshwater lakes, rivers and marshes.

Similar Birds

Common Tern

Caspian Tern

Least Tern

no black cap

nonbreeding

black cap and nape

large, orange, black-tipped bill

long tail projects beyond wing tips

pure white underparts

orange legs

breeding

Nesting: does not nest in Missouri; nests locally throughout North America; occasionally colonial; a platform of floating vegetation in a marsh; darkly blotched, olive to buff eggs are 1⅝ x 1¼ in; pair incubates 2–3 eggs for 24 days.

Did You Know?

The Forster's Tern's bill color changes from black in winter to orange with a black tip in summer.

Look For

Like most terns, Forster's Tern catches fish in dramatic head-first dives, but also snatches flying insects in midair.

Rock Pigeon
Columba livia

Rock Pigeons are familiar to most anyone who has lived in the city. These colorful, acrobatic, seed-eating birds frequent parks, town squares, railroad yards and factory sites. Their tolerance of humans has made them a source of entertainment, as well as a pest. • This pigeon is likely a descendant of a Eurasian bird that was first domesticated about 4500 BC. The Rock Pigeon was introduced to North America in the 17th century by settlers. Much of our understanding of bird migration, endocrinology, color genetics and sensory perception comes from experiments involving Rock Pigeons, the most well-studied birds in the world.

Other ID: *In flight:* holds wings in a deep "V" while gliding.
Size: L 12–13 in; W 28 in (male is usually larger).
Voice: soft, cooing *coorrr-coorrr-coorrr*.
Status: common permanent resident.
Habitat: urban areas, railroad yards and agricultural areas; high cliffs often provide more natural habitat.

Similar Birds

Mourning Dove (p. 68)

Eurasian Collared-Dove

color is highly variable
(iridescent blue-gray,
red, white or tan)

usually has
white rump

white cere

feet usually orangy red

Nesting: in a barn or on a cliff, bridge or tower; in a flimsy nest of sticks, grass and other vegetation; glossy white eggs are 1½ x 1⅛ in; pair incubates 2 eggs for 16–19 days; may raise broods year-round.

Did You Know?

Both Caesar and Napoleon used Rock Pigeons as message couriers.

Look For

No other "wild" bird varies as much in coloration, a result of semidomestication and extensive inbreeding over time.

Mourning Dove

Zenaida macroura

The Mourning Dove's soft cooing, which filters through broken woodlands and suburban parks, is often confused with the sound of a hooting owl. Beginning birders who track down the source of the calls are often surprised to find the streamlined silhouette of a perched dove. • This popular game animal is one of the most abundant native birds in North America. Its numbers and range have increased as human development has created more open habitats and food sources, such as waste grain and bird feeders.

Other ID: buffy, gray-brown plumage; small head; dark bill; sleek body; dull red legs.
Size: L 11–13 in; W 18 in.
Voice: mournful, soft, slow *oh-woe-woe-woe*.
Status: common permanent resident.
Habitat: open and riparian woodlands, forest edges, agricultural and suburban areas, open parks.

Similar Birds

Rock Pigeon (p. 66)

Eurasian Collared-Dove

pale blue
eye ring

dark, shiny patch
below ear

black spots on
upperwing

pale rosy
underparts

long, white-
trimmed,
tapering tail

Nesting: in a shrub or tree; occasionally on the ground; nest is a fragile, shallow platform of twigs; white eggs are 1⅛ x ⅞ in; pair incubates 2 eggs for 14 days.

Did You Know?

The Mourning Dove raises up to six broods each year—more than any other native bird.

Look For

When the Mourning Dove bursts into flight, its wings clap above and below its body. You may also hear a whistling sound as this bird flies at high speed.

Yellow-billed Cuckoo
Coccyzus americanus

Large tracts of hardwood forest and riparian areas provide valuable habitat for the Yellow-billed Cuckoo, a bird that is declining or has disappeared in some states. Songbirds are increasingly vulnerable to predators in the patchy, fragmented forests left behind by human development. The cuckoo's habitat has also deteriorated over the years as waterways have been altered or dammed. • Most of the time, the Yellow-billed Cuckoo lives silently within impenetrable, deciduous undergrowth, relying on obscurity for survival. Then, for a short period during nesting, the male cuckoo tempts fate by issuing a barrage of loud, rhythmic courtship calls.

Other ID: olive brown upperparts; white underparts.
Size: L 11–13 in; W 18 in.
Voice: long series of deep, hollow *kuks,* slowing near the end: *kuk-kuk-kuk-kuk kuk kop kow kowlp kowlp.*
Status: fairly common migrant and summer resident.
Habitat: semi-open deciduous habitats; dense tangles and thickets at the edges of orchards, urban parks, agricultural fields and roadways; sometimes woodlots.

Similar Birds

Black-billed Cuckoo

Mourning Dove (p. 68)

yellow eye ring

rufous tinge on
primaries

mainly yellow,
downcurved bill
with black upper
ridge

long tail with large
white spots on
underside

Nesting: on a low horizontal branch in a deciduous shrub or small tree; flimsy platform nest of
twigs is lined with grass; pale bluish green eggs are
1¼ x ⅞ in; pair incubates 3–4 eggs for 9–11 days.

Did You Know?

Yellow-billed Cuckoos lay
larger clutches when
cyclical outbreaks of
cicadas or tent caterpil-
lars provide an abundant
food supply.

Look For

Also known as "Rain Crow,"
the Yellow-billed Cuckoo has a
propensity for calling on dark,
cloudy days and a reputation
for predicting rainstorms.

Eastern Screech-Owl
Megascops asio

red morph

The diminutive Eastern Screech-Owl is a year-round resident of low-elevation, deciduous woodlands, but it is rarely detected. Most screech-owls sleep away the daylight hours snuggled safely inside tree cavities, artificial nest boxes or conifers, especially small red-cedars. • A mobbing horde of chickadees or a squawking gang of Blue Jays can alert you to an owl's presence during the day. Smaller birds that mob a screech-owl often do so after losing a family member during the night. • Unique among Missouri owls, Eastern Screech-Owls show both red and gray color morphs. In Missouri, the gray morph is more common. Very rarely, an intermediate brown morph occurs.

Other ID: reddish or grayish overall; yellow eyes.
Size: *L* 8–9 in; *W* 20–22 in.
Voice: horselike "whinny" that rises and falls.
Status: common permanent resident.
Habitat: mature deciduous forests, open deciduous and riparian woodlands, orchards and shade trees with natural cavities.

Similar Birds

Northern
Saw-whet Owl

Long-eared Owl

short "ear" tufts

pale grayish bill

dark breast streaking

gray morph

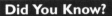

Nesting: in a natural cavity or artificial nest box; no lining is added; white eggs are 1½ x 1⅜ in; female incubates 4–5 eggs for about 26 days; male brings food to the female during incubation.

Did You Know?

Screech-owls have one of the most varied diets of any owl, capturing small animals, earthworms, insects and sometimes even snagging fish from creeks.

Look For

Eastern Screech-Owls respond readily to whistled imitations of their calls, and sometimes several owls will appear to investigate the fraudulent perpetrator.

Great Horned Owl
Bubo virginianus

This highly adaptable and superbly camouflaged hunter has sharp hearing and powerful vision, which allow it to hunt at night as well as by day. It will swoop down from a perch onto almost any small creature that moves. • An owl has specially designed feathers on its wings to reduce noise. The leading edges of the flight feathers are fringed rather than smooth, which interrupts airflow over the wing and allows the owl to fly noiselessly. • Great Horned Owls begin their courtship as early as January, and by February and March, the females are already incubating their eggs.

Other ID: overall plumage varies from light gray to dark brown; heavily mottled, gray, brown and black upperparts; yellow eyes; white "chin."
Size: L 18–25 in; W 3–5 ft.
Voice: breeding call is 4–6 deep hoots: *hoo-hoo-hoooo hoo-hoo* or *Who's awake? Me too;* female gives higher-pitched hoots.
Status: fairly common permanent resident.
Habitat: fragmented forests, fields, riparian woodlands, suburban parks and wooded edges of clearings.

Similar Birds

Long-eared Owl

Barred Owl (p. 76)

tall, widely spaced
"ear" tufts form a
triangle with beak

rusty orange facial
disc is outlined in
black

fine, horizontal
barring on breast

Nesting: in another bird's abandoned stick nest
or in a tree cavity; adds little or no nest material;
dull whitish eggs are 2¼ x 1⅞ in; mostly the
female incubates 2–3 eggs for 28–35 days.

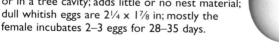

Did You Know?

The Great Horned Owl
has a poor sense of smell,
which might explain why it
is the only consistent
predator of skunks.

Look For

Owls regurgitate pellets that
contain the indigestible parts
of their prey. You can find
these pellets, which are generally clean and dry, under
frequently used perches.

Barred Owl
Strix varia

The adaptable Barred Owl is found in many woodland habitats throughout Missouri, especially those near water. It uses large tracts of mature forest, ranging from swampy bottomlands to higher, mixed forests. • Each spring, the escalating laughs, hoots and gargling howls of Barred Owls reinforce pair bonds. They tend to be most vocal during late evening and early morning when the moon is full, the air is calm and the sky is clear.

Other ID: mottled, dark gray-brown plumage.
Size: *L* 17–24 in; *W* 3½–4 ft.
Voice: loud, hooting, rhythmic, laughlike call is heard mostly in spring: *Who cooks for you? Who cooks for you all?*
Status: common permanent resident.
Habitat: mature coniferous and mixedwood forests, especially in dense stands near swamps, streams and lakes.

Similar Birds

Great Horned Owl
(p. 74)

Short-eared Owl

no "ear" tufts

dark eyes

pale bill

horizontal barring
around neck and
upper breast

vertical streaking
on belly

Nesting: in a natural tree cavity, broken treetop
or abandoned stick nest; adds very little material
to the nest; white eggs are 2 x 1⅝ in; female
incubates 2–3 eggs for 28–33 days.

Did You Know?

In darkness, the Barred
Owl's eyesight may be 100
times keener than that of
humans, and it can locate
and follow prey using
sound alone.

Look For

Dark eyes make the Barred
Owl unique—most familiar
large owls in North America
have yellow eyes.

Common Nighthawk
Chordeiles minor

The Common Nighthawk makes an unforgettable booming sound as it flies high overhead. In an energetic courting display, the male dives, then swerves skyward, making a hollow *vroom* sound with its wings. • Like other members of the nightjar family, the Common Nighthawk has adapted to catch insects in midair: its large gaping mouth is surrounded by feather shafts that funnel insects into its bill. A nighthawk can eat over 2600 insects in one day, including mosquitoes, blackflies and flying ants. • Look for Common Nighthawks foraging for insects at nighttime baseball games.

Other ID: *In flight:* shallowly forked, barred tail; erratic flight.
Size: *L* 8–10 in; *W* 23–26 in.
Voice: frequently repeated, nasal *peent peent;* wings make a deep, hollow *vroom* during courtship dives.
Status: common summer resident.
Habitat: *Breeding:* forest openings, bogs, rocky outcroppings and gravel rooftops.
In migration: often near water; any area with large numbers of flying insects.

Similar Birds

Chuck-will's-widow

Whip-poor-will
(p. 80)

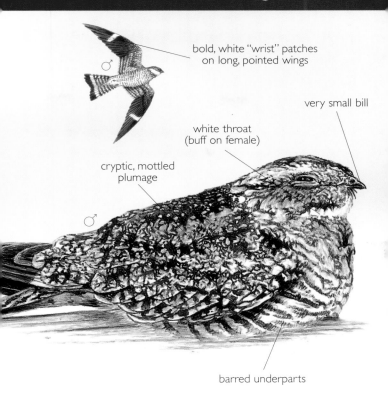

bold, white "wrist" patches
on long, pointed wings

very small bill

white throat
(buff on female)

cryptic, mottled
plumage

♂

♂

barred underparts

Nesting: on bare ground; no nest is built; heavily marked, creamy white to buff eggs are 1⅛ x ⅞ in; female incubates 2 eggs for about 19 days; both adults feed the young.

Did You Know?

It was once believed that members of the nightjar, or "goatsucker," family could suck milk from the udders of goats, causing the goats to go blind!

Look For

With their short legs and tiny feet, nighthawks sit lengthwise on tree branches and blend in perfectly with the bark.

Whip-poor-will

Caprimulgus vociferus

These magical, elusive birds blend seamlessly into lichen-covered bark or the forest floor. On spring evenings, their airy, soothing *whip-poor-will* calls float through the open woodlands, signaling to prospective mates. • Ground-nesting Whip-poor-wills time their egg-laying to the lunar cycle so that hatchlings can be fed more efficiently during the light of the full moon. For the first 20 days after hatching, until the young are able to fly, the parents feed them regurgitated insects.

Other ID: mottled, brown-gray overall with black flecking; large eyes; dark throat; relatively long, rounded tail. *Red morph:* mottled, rufous overall; pale gray markings on wings.
Size: *L* 9–10 in; *W* 16–20 in.
Voice: whistled *whip-poor-will*, with emphasis on the *will*.
Status: common summer resident.
Habitat: open deciduous and pine woodlands; often along forest edges.

Similar Birds

Chuck-will's-widow

Common Nighthawk
(p. 78)

white outer tail feathers
(buff on female)

♂

rounded
wings

dark stripe runs down
center of crown

♂

dark throat

white "necklace"
(buff on female)

Nesting: on the ground in leaf or pine needle litter; no nest is built; brown-blotched, whitish eggs are 1¼ x ⅞ in; female incubates 2 eggs for 19–20 days; both adults raise the young.

Did You Know?

Within days of hatching, young Whip-poor-wills can scurry away from their nest in search of protective cover if disturbed.

Look For

Cryptic plumage, sleepy daytime habits and secretive nesting behavior mean a hopeful observer must literally stumble upon a Whip-poor-will to see one.

Chimney Swift
Chaetura pelagica

Chimney Swifts are the "frequent fliers" of the bird world—they feed, drink, bathe, collect nest material and even mate while they fly! They spend much of their time catching insects in the skies above the treetops. During night migrations, swifts sleep as they fly, relying on changing wind conditions to steer them. • Chimney Swifts have small, weak legs and cannot take flight again if they land on the ground. For this reason, swifts usually cling to vertical surfaces with their strong claws.

Other ID: brown overall; slim body. *In flight:* rapid wingbeats; boomerang-shaped profile; erratic flight pattern.
Size: L 5–5½ in; W 12–13 in.
Voice: call is a rapid *chitter-chitter-chitter,* given in flight; also gives a rapid series of staccato *chip* notes.
Status: common migrant and summer resident.
Habitat: forages above cities and towns; roosts and nests in chimneys; may nest in tree cavities in more remote areas.

Similar Birds

Northern Rough-winged Swallow (p. 118)

Bank Swallow

Cliff Swallow

long, thin, pointed, crescent-shaped wings

squared tail

Nesting: often colonial; half-saucer nest of short twigs is attached to a vertical wall using saliva; white eggs are ¾ x ½ in; pair incubates 4–5 eggs for 19–21 days.

Did You Know?

Migrating Chimney Swifts may fly as high as 10,000 feet—above this altitude aircraft are required to carry oxygen.

Look For

In early evenings during migration, Chimney Swifts are often seen in large numbers swirling above large, old chimneys before they enter to roost for the night.

Ruby-throated Hummingbird

Archilochus colubris

Ruby-throated Hummingbirds bridge the ecological gap between birds and bees—they feed on sweet, energy-rich flower nectar and pollinate flowers in the process. You can attract hummingbirds to your backyard with a red nectar feeder filled with a sugar-water solution (red food coloring is both unnecessary and harmful to the birds) or native nectar-producing flowers such as honeysuckle or bee balm.
• Each year, Ruby-throated Hummingbirds migrate across the Gulf of Mexico—a nonstop, 500-mile journey.

Other ID: thin, needlelike bill; pale underparts.
Female: green-gold crown and back; white underparts.
Nonbreeding male: dark brown to black throat.
Immature: similar to female.
Size: L 3½–4 in; W 4–4½ in.
Voice: a loud *chick* and other high squeaks; soft buzzing of the wings while in flight.
Status: common summer resident.
Habitat: open, mixed woodlands, wetlands, orchards, tree-lined meadows, flower gardens and backyards with trees and feeders.

Similar Birds

Rufous Hummingbird

Look For

A hummingbird with a greenish back and white throat is likely a female Ruby-throated Hummingbird. Nonbreeding males have dark brown to black throats.

fine, dark streaking
on white throat

iridescent,
green back

♀

black "chin" and
ruby red throat

dark tail with
white tips

♂

dark tail

Nesting: on a horizontal tree limb; tiny, deep cup
nest of plant down and fibers is held together
with spider silk; lichens and leaves are pasted on
the exterior walls; white eggs are $\frac{1}{2}$ x $\frac{3}{8}$ in;
female incubates 2 eggs for 13–16 days.

Did You Know?

In straight-ahead flight, hummingbirds beat their wings up to
80 times per second, and their hearts can beat up to 1200
times per minute! Weighing about as much as a nickel, a hummingbird can briefly reach speeds of up to 60 miles per hour.

Belted Kingfisher
Ceryle alcyon

Perched on a bare branch over a productive pool, the Belted Kingfisher utters a scratchy, rattling call. Then, with little regard for its scruffy hairdo, the "king of the fishers" plunges headfirst into the water to snatch a fish or a frog. Back on land, the kingfisher flips its prey into the air and swallows it headfirst. Similar to owls, kingfishers regurgitate the indigestible portion of their food as pellets, which can be found beneath favorite perches. • Nestlings have closed eyes and are featherless for the first week, but after five days they can swallow small fish whole. The adults feed nestlings up to eight small fish each day.

Other ID: bluish upperparts; small, white patch near eye; straight bill; short legs; white underwings.
Size: L 11–14 in; W 20–21 in.
Voice: fast, repetitive, cackling rattle, like a teacup shaking on a saucer.
Status: fairly common permanent resident; less common in winter.
Habitat: rivers, large streams, lakes, marshes and beaver ponds, especially near exposed soil banks, gravel pits or bluffs.

Similar Birds

Blue Jay (p. 110)

Look For

The Belted Kingfisher often flies very close to the water, so close, in fact, that its wing tips may skim the surface.

shaggy crest

white "collar"

♀

rust-colored "belt"
on female may be
incomplete

♂

blue-gray
breast band

Nesting: in a cavity at the end of an earth
burrow; glossy white eggs are 1⅜ x 1 in; pair
incubates 6–7 eggs for 22–24 days.

Did You Know?

During the breeding season, a pair of kingfishers typically
takes turns excavating the nest burrow, which is usually on
a sandy bank near water. They use their sturdy bills and claws
to dig burrows that may measure up to 6 feet long.

Red-headed Woodpecker
Melanerpes erythrocephalus

This bird of the East lives mostly in open deciduous woodlands, urban parks and oak savannahs. Red-headed Woodpeckers were once common through-out their range, but their numbers have declined dramatically over the past century. Since the intro-duction of the European Starling, Red-heads have been largely outcompeted for nesting cavities.

• These birds are frequent traffic fatalities. They are often struck by vehicles when they dart from their perches and over roadways to catch flying insects.

Other ID: black back, wings and tail; white underparts. *Juvenile:* slight brown streaking on white underparts.
Size: L 9–9½ in; W 17 in.
Voice: loud series of *kweer* or *kwrring* notes; occa-sionally a chattering *kerr-r-ruck;* also drums softly in short bursts.
Status: fairly common summer resident; less common in winter.
Habitat: open deciduous woodlands (espe-cially oak woodlands), urban parks, river edges and roadsides with groves of scattered trees.

Similar Birds

Red-bellied Woodpecker (p. 90)

Pileated Woodpecker (p. 96)

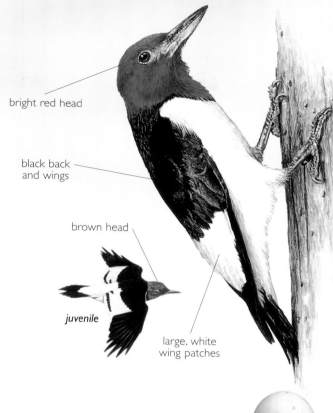

bright red head

black back
and wings

brown head

juvenile

large, white
wing patches

Nesting: male excavates a nest cavity in a dead tree or limb; white eggs are 1 x ¾ in; pair incubates 4–5 eggs for 12–13 days; both adults feed the young.

Did You Know?

The Red-headed Woodpecker is one of only four woodpecker species that regularly caches food.

Look For

The forested bottomlands, swamps and semi-open habitats of northern Missouri are favorite haunts of this charismatic bird.

Red-bellied Woodpecker
Melanerpes carolinus

The familiar Red-bellied Woodpecker is no stranger to suburban backyards and will sometimes nest in birdhouses. This widespread bird is found year-round in woodlands throughout the eastern states, but numbers fluctuate depending on habitat availability and weather conditions. • Unlike most woodpeckers, Red-bellies consume large amounts of plant material, seldom excavating wood for insects. • When occupying an area together with Red-headed Woodpeckers, Red-bellies will nest in the trunk, below the foliage, and the Red-heads will nest in dead branches among the foliage.

Other ID: reddish tinge on belly. *Juvenile:* dark gray crown; streaked breast.
Size: *L* 9–10½ in; *W* 16 in.
Voice: call is a soft, rolling *churr;* drums in second-long bursts.
Status: common permanent resident.
Habitat: mature deciduous woodlands; occasionally in wooded residential areas.

Similar Birds

Northern Flicker
(p. 94)

Yellow-bellied
Sapsucker

Red-headed
Woodpecker (p. 88)

red nape extends to forehead

black and white barring on back

red on nape only

♂

♀

white patches on rump and topside base of primaries

Nesting: in a woodland or residential area; in a cavity excavated mainly by the male; white eggs are 1 x ¾ in; pair incubates 4–5 eggs for 12–14 days.

Did You Know?

Studies of banded Red-bellied Woodpeckers have shown that these birds may have a lifespan in the wild of more than 20 years.

Look For

The Red-bellied Woodpecker's namesake, its red belly, is only a small reddish area that is difficult to see in the field.

Downy Woodpecker

Picoides pubescens

A bird feeder well stocked with peanut butter and black-oil sunflower seeds may attract a pair of Downy Woodpeckers to your backyard. These approachable little birds are more tolerant of human activity than most other species, and they visit feeders more often than the larger, more aggressive Hairy Woodpeckers *(P. villosus).* • Like other woodpeckers, the Downy has evolved special features to help cushion the shock of repeated hammering, including a strong bill and neck muscles, a flexible, reinforced skull and a brain that is tightly packed in its protective cranium.

Other ID: black eye line and crown; white belly. *Male:* small, red patch on back of head. *Female:* no red patch.
Size: *L* 6–7 in; *W* 12 in.
Voice: long, unbroken trill; calls are a sharp *pik* or *ki-ki-ki* or whiny *queek queek.*
Status: common permanent resident.
Habitat: any wooded environment, especially deciduous and mixed forests and areas with tall, deciduous shrubs.

Similar Birds

Hairy Woodpecker

Yellow-bellied
Sapsucker

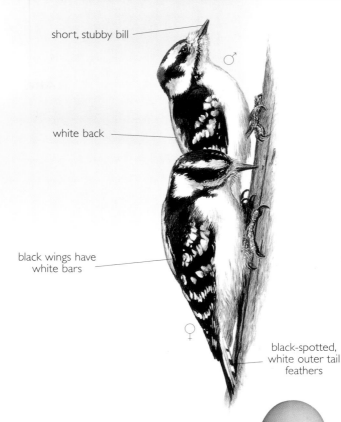

short, stubby bill ♂

white back

black wings have
white bars

♀

black-spotted,
white outer tail
feathers

Nesting: pair excavates a cavity in a dying or
decaying trunk and lines it with wood chips;
white eggs are ¾ x ⅝ in; pair incubates 4–5 eggs
for 11–13 days.

Did You Know?

Woodpeckers have feath-
ered nostrils that filter
out the sawdust produced
by hammering.

Look For

Both Downy Woodpeckers
and Hairy Woodpeckers have
white outer tail feathers, but
the Downy's have several
dark spots while the Hairy's
are pure white.

Northern Flicker
Colaptes auratus

Instead of boring holes in trees, the Northern Flicker scours the ground in search of invertebrates, particularly ants. With robinlike hops, it investigates anthills, grassy meadows and forest clearings. • Flickers often bathe in dusty depressions. The dust particles absorb oils and bacteria that can harm the birds' feathers. To clean themselves even more thoroughly, flickers squash captured ants and preen themselves with the remains. Ants contain formic acid, which kills small parasites on the flickers' skin and feathers.

Other ID: long bill; brownish to buff face; gray crown; white rump. *Male:* black "mustache" stripe. *Female:* no "mustache."
Size: L 12–13 in; W 20 in.
Voice: loud, rapid, laughlike *kick-kick-kick-kick-kick-kick; woika-woika-woika* issued during courtship.
Status: common permanent resident; less common in winter.
Habitat: *Breeding:* open woodlands and forest edges, fields, meadows, beaver ponds and other wetlands. *In migration* and *winter:* coastal vegetation, offshore islands, urban gardens.

Similar Birds

Red-bellied
Woodpecker (p. 90)

Yellow-bellied
Sapsucker

brown, black-barred back and wings

"Yellow-shafted Flicker"

♂

black-spotted, buff to whitish underparts

red nape crescent

black "bib"

♀

yellow underwings and undertail

Nesting: pair excavates a cavity in a dying or decaying trunk and lines it with wood chips; may also use a nest box; white eggs are 1⅛ x ⅞ in; pair incubates 5–8 eggs for 11–16 days.

Did You Know?

The very long tongue of a woodpecker wraps around twin structures in the skull and is stored like a measuring tape in its case.

Look For

Northern Flickers prefer to forage at anthills and may visit their favorite colonies regularly, hammering and probing into the ground to unearth adults and larvae.

Pileated Woodpecker
Dryocopus pileatus

The Pileated Woodpecker, with its flaming red crest, chisel-like bill and commanding size, requires 100 acres of mature forest as a home territory. In Missouri, the patchwork of woodlots and small towns limits the availability of continuous habitat, requiring this woodpecker to show itself more.

• A pair will spend up to six weeks excavating a large nest cavity in a dead or decaying tree. Wood Ducks, kestrels, owls and even flying squirrels frequently nest in abandoned Pileated Woodpecker cavities.

Other ID: predominantly black; yellow eyes; white "chin." *Male:* red "mustache." *Female:* no red "mustache"; gray-brown forehead.
Size: L 16–17 in; W 28–29 in.
Voice: loud, fast, rolling *woika-woika-woika-woika;* long series of *kuk* notes; loud, resonant drumming.
Status: fairly common permanent resident in southern Missouri; rare in the north.
Habitat: extensive tracts of mature forests; also riparian woodlands or woodlots in suburban and agricultural areas.

Similar Birds

Red-headed
Woodpecker (p. 88)

Ivory-billed
Woodpecker

flaming red crest extends farther on male ♂

stout, dark bill

white stripe runs from bill to shoulder

♀

white wing linings

Nesting: pair excavates a cavity in a dying or decaying trunk and lines it with wood chips; white eggs are 1¼ x 1 in; pair incubates 4 eggs for 15–18 days.

Did You Know?

A woodpecker's bill becomes shorter as the bird ages, so juvenile birds have slightly longer bills than adults.

Look For

Foraging Pileated Woodpeckers leave large rectangular cavities up to 12 inches long near the base of trees.

Eastern Wood-Pewee
Contopus virens

Our most common and widespread woodland fly-catcher, the Eastern Wood-Pewee, breeds in every county in Missouri. The male's plaintive, whistled *pee-ah-wee pee-oh* song is repeated all day long throughout summer. Some males will even sing their charms late into the evening, long after most birds have silenced their weary courtship songs. • Many insects have evolved defense mechanisms to avert potential predators such as the Eastern Wood-Pewee and other flycatchers. Some flying insects are camouflaged, and others are distasteful or poisonous and flaunt their foul nature with vivid colors.

Other ID: slender body; olive gray to olive brown upperparts; whitish throat; gray breast and sides; whitish or pale yellow belly, flanks and undertail coverts.
Size: *L* 6–6½ in; *W* 10 in.
Voice: *Male:* song is a clear, slow, plaintive *pee-ah-wee*, with the 2nd note lower, followed by a down-slurred *pee-oh*; also a *chip* call.
Status: abundant summer resident.
Habitat: open, mixed and deciduous woodlands with a sparse understory, especially woodland openings and edges; rarely in open coniferous woodlands.

Similar Birds

Olive-sided Flycatcher

Eastern Phoebe
(p. 102)

Eastern Kingbird
(p. 106)

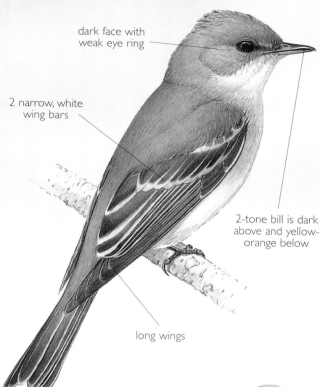

dark face with weak eye ring

2 narrow, white wing bars

2-tone bill is dark above and yellow-orange below

long wings

Nesting: on a horizontal branch in a deciduous tree, well away from the trunk; open cup nest of plants and lichen is bound with spider silk; darkly blotched, whitish eggs are $^{11}/_{16}$ x $^{9}/_{16}$ in; female incubates 3 eggs for 12–13 days.

Did You Know?

Sometimes you can hear the snap of a wood-pewee's bill closing around an insect.

Look For

Like other flycatchers, the Eastern Wood-Pewee loops out from an exposed perch to snatch flying insects in midair, a technique often referred to as "flycatching" or "hawking."

Acadian Flycatcher
Empidonax virescens

The Acadian Flycatcher's quick, forceful *peet-sa* song is one of its key features, but learning to identify this bird is only half the fun. Its speedy, aerial courtship chases and the male's hovering flight displays are sights to behold—that is if you can survive the swarming hordes of bloodsucking mosquitoes deep within the swampy woodlands where this flycatcher is primarily found. • Maple and beech trees provide preferred nest sites for the Acadian Flycatcher. The nest is built on a horizontal branch up to 20 feet above the ground and can be quite conspicuous because loose material often dangles from the nest.

Other ID: large bill has dark upper mandible and pinkish yellow lower mandible; faint olive yellow breast; yellow belly and undertail coverts.
Size: L 5½–6 in; W 9 in.
Voice: song is a forceful *peet-sa;* call is a softer *peet;* may issue a loud, flickerlike *ti-ti-ti-ti-ti* during the breeding season.
Status: common summer resident in southern Missouri; uncommon in the north.
Habitat: fairly mature deciduous woodlands, riparian woodlands and wooded swamps.

Similar Birds

Alder Flycatcher   Willow Flycatcher   Least Flycatcher   Yellow-bellied Flycatcher

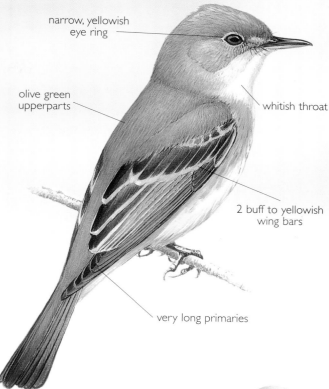

narrow, yellowish eye ring

olive green upperparts

whitish throat

2 buff to yellowish wing bars

very long primaries

Nesting: low in a deciduous tree; female builds a loose cup nest from vegetation held together with spider silk; lightly spotted, creamy white eggs are 11/16 x 9/16 in; female incubates 3 eggs for 13–15 days.

Did You Know?

Flycatchers are members of the family *Tyrannidae*, or "Tyrant Flycatchers," so named because of their feisty, aggressive behavior.

Look For

A standing dead tree or "planted" tree limb in your backyard may attract flycatchers that are looking for a hunting perch.

Eastern Phoebe

Sayornis phoebe

Whether you are poking around a barnyard, a campground picnic shelter or your backyard shed, there is a very good chance you will stumble upon an Eastern Phoebe family and its marvelous mud nest. The Eastern Phoebe's nest-building and territorial defense is normally well underway by the time most other songbirds arrive in Missouri in mid-May. Once limited to nesting on natural cliffs and fallen riparian trees, this adaptive flycatcher has found success nesting in culverts and under bridges and eaves, especially when water is near.

Other ID: gray-brown upperparts; belly may be washed with yellow in fall; no eye ring; no obvious wing bars; dark legs.
Size: L 6½–7 in; W 10½ in.
Voice: *Male:* song is a hearty, snappy *fee-bee*, delivered frequently; call is a sharp *chip*.
Status: common summer resident.
Habitat: open deciduous woodlands, forest edges and clearings; usually near water.

Similar Birds

Eastern Wood-Pewee
(p. 98)

Acadian Flycatcher
(p. 100)

Eastern Kingbird
(p. 106)

dark head and bill

gray wash on
breast and sides

white underparts

breeding

frequently
pumps its tail

Nesting: under the ledge of a building, picnic shelter, bridge, cliff or well; cup-shaped mud nest is lined with soft material; unmarked, white eggs are ¾ x ⁹/₁₆ in; female incubates 4–5 eggs for about 16 days.

Did You Know?

Eastern Phoebes sometimes reuse their nest sites for many years. Females that save energy by reusing their nests can often lay more eggs.

Look For

Some other birds pump their tails while perched, but few species can match the zest and frequency of the Eastern Phoebe's tail pumping.

Great Crested Flycatcher

Myiarchus crinitus

Loud, raucous calls give away the presence of the brightly colored Great Crested Flycatcher. This large flycatcher often inhabits forest edges and nests in woodlands throughout Missouri. Unlike other eastern flycatchers, the Great Crested prefers to nest in a natural tree cavity or abandoned woodpecker hole, or sometimes uses a nest box intended for a bluebird. Once in a while, the Great Crested Flycatcher will decorate the nest entrance with a shed snakeskin or substitute translucent plastic wrap. The purpose of this practice is not fully understood, though it might make any would-be predators think twice.

Other ID: dark olive brown upperparts; heavy black bill.
Size: *L* 8–9 in; *W* 13 in.
Voice: loud, whistled *wheep!* and a rolling *prrrrreet!*
Status: common summer resident.
Habitat: deciduous and mixed woodlands and forests, usually near openings or edges.

Similar Birds

Acadian Flycatcher
(p. 100)

Eastern Kingbird
(p. 106)

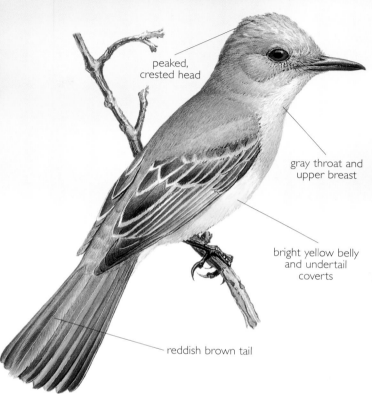

peaked, crested head

gray throat and upper breast

bright yellow belly and undertail coverts

reddish brown tail

Nesting: in a tree cavity or artificial cavity lined with grass; may hang a shed snakeskin over entrance hole; heavily marked, creamy white to pale buff eggs are ⅞ x ⅝ in; female incubates 5 eggs for 13–15 days.

Did You Know?

Many animals depend on tree cavities for shelter and nesting, so instead of cutting down large, dead trees, consider leaving a few standing.

Look For

Follow the loud *wheep!* calls and watch for a show of bright yellow and rufous feathers to find this flycatcher.

Eastern Kingbird

Tyrannus tyrannus

Sometimes referred to as the "Jekyll and Hyde" bird, the Eastern Kingbird is a gregarious fruit eater while wintering in South America and an anti-social, aggressive insect eater while nesting in North America. The Eastern Kingbird fearlessly attacks crows, hawks and even humans that pass through its territory, pursuing and pecking at them until the threat has passed. No one familiar with the Eastern Kingbird's pugnacious behavior will refute its scientific name, *Tyrannus tyrannus*. This bird reveals a gentler side of its character in a quivering, butterfly-like courtship flight.

Other ID: black bill and legs; no eye ring; white underparts; grayish breast.
Size: *L* 8½–9 in; W 15 in.
Voice: call is a quick, loud, chattering *kit-kit-kitter-kitter;* also a buzzy *dzee-dzee-dzee.*
Status: common summer resident.
Habitat: fields with scattered shrubs, trees or hedgerows, forest fringes, clearings, shrubby roadsides, towns and farmyards.

Similar Birds

Eastern Phoebe (p. 102)

Look For

Eastern Kingbirds are common and widespread. On a drive in the country you will likely spot at least one of these birds sitting on a fence or utility wire.

small head crest

thin, orange-red
crown (rarely seen)

dark gray to black
upperparts

white-tipped tail

Nesting: on a horizontal limb, stump or
upturned tree root; cup nest is made of weeds,
twigs and grass; darkly blotched, white to pinkish
eggs are 1 x ¾ in; female incubates 3–4 eggs for
14–18 days.

Did You Know?

For an Eastern Kingbird, bathing involves repeatedly flying
close enough to the surface of the water to wet its head
and breast. Then it settles on a perch to preen itself.

Red-eyed Vireo

Vireo olivaceus

Capable of delivering about 40 phrases per minute, the male Red-eyed Vireo can out-sing any one of his courting neighbors. One tenacious male set a record by singing 21,000 phrases in one day! Although you may still hear the Red-eyed Vireo singing five or six hours after other songbirds have ceased for the day, this bird is not easy to spot. It is usually concealed in its olive brown plumage among the foliage of deciduous trees. Its unique red eyes, unusual among songbirds, are even trickier to spot without a good pair of binoculars. • Look for this bird in Ozark forests.

Other ID: black-bordered, olive "cheek"; olive green upperparts; white to pale gray underparts.
Size: L 6 in; W 10 in.
Voice: call is a short, scolding *rreeah*.
Male: song is a series of quick, continuous, variable phrases with pauses in between: *look-up, way-up, tree-top, see-me, here-I-am!*
Status: abundant summer resident.
Habitat: deciduous or mixed woodlands with a shrubby understory.

Similar Birds

White-eyed Vireo   Warbling Vireo   Tennessee Warbler

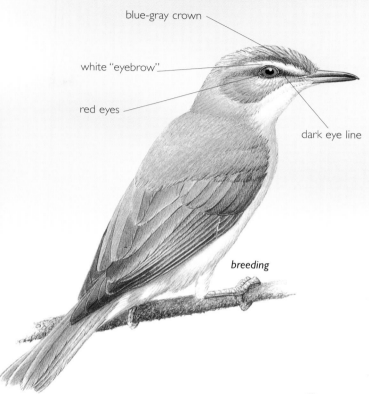

blue-gray crown

white "eyebrow"

red eyes

dark eye line

breeding

Nesting: in a tree or shrub; hanging cup nest is made of grass, roots, spider silk and cocoons; darkly spotted, white eggs are ¾ x ½ in; female incubates 4 eggs for 11–14 days.

Did You Know?

If a Brown-headed Cowbird parasitizes its nest, a Red-eyed Vireo will respond by abandoning the nest or by raising the cowbird young with its own.

Look For

The Red-eyed Vireo perches with a hunched stance and hops with its body turned diagonally to its direction of travel.

Blue Jay

Cyanocitta cristata

The Blue Jay is the only member of the corvid family in Missouri that is dressed in blue. White-flecked wing feathers and sharply defined facial features make the Blue Jay easy to recognize. • Jays can be quite aggressive when competing for sunflower seeds and peanuts at backyard feeding stations and rarely hesitate to drive away smaller birds, squirrels or even threatening cats. Even the Great Horned Owl is not too formidable a predator for a group of these brave, boisterous mobsters to harass.

Other ID: blue upperparts; white underparts; black bill.
Size: *L* 11–12 in; *W* 16 in.
Voice: noisy, screaming *jay-jay-jay;* nasal *queedle queedle queedle-queedle* sounds like a muted trumpet; often imitates various sounds, including calls of other birds.
Status: common permanent resident.
Habitat: mixed deciduous forests, agricultural areas, scrubby fields and townsites.

Similar Birds

Belted Kingfisher
(p. 86)

Eastern Bluebird
(p. 130)

blue crest

black "necklace"

white bar and
flecking on wings

dark bars and white
corners on blue tail

Nesting: in a tree or tall shrub; pair builds
a bulky stick nest; greenish, buff or pale eggs,
spotted with gray and brown are 1⅛ x ¾ in;
pair incubates 4–5 eggs for 16–18 days.

Did You Know?

Blue Jays store food from
feeders in trees and other
places for later use.

Look For

When you hear the call of a
Red-tailed Hawk, an American
Crow or even a neighbor-
hood cat, make sure it is not
really a Blue Jay imitating
their calls.

American Crow
Corvus brachyrhynchos

The noise that most often emanates from this treetop squawker seems unrepresentative of its intelligence. However, this wary, clever bird is also an impressive mimic, able to whine like a dog and laugh or cry like a human. • American Crows have flourished in spite of considerable efforts, over many generations, to reduce their numbers. One of the reasons for this species' staying power is that it is a generalist, which allows it to adapt to a variety of habitats, food types and changing environmental conditions.

Other ID: glossy, purple-black plumage; black bill and legs; rounded wings in flight.
Size: *L* 17–21 in; *W* 3 ft.
Voice: distinctive, far-carrying, repetitive *caw-caw-caw*.
Status: common permanent resident.
Habitat: urban areas, agricultural fields and other open areas with scattered woodlands.

Similar Birds

Common Raven

Common Grackle

slim, sleek head
and throat

short, square-
shaped tail

Nesting: in a tree or on a utility pole; large stick-
and-branch nest is lined with fur and soft plant
material; darkly blotched, gray-green to blue-
green eggs are 1⅝ x 1⅛ in; female incubates
4–6 eggs for about 18 days.

Did You Know?

Crows are family oriented,
and the young from the
previous year may help
their parents to raise the
nestlings.

Look For

The American Crow has a
square tail and a slimmer bill
than the larger but similar-
looking Common Raven.

Horned Lark
Eremophila alpestris

Performing an impressive, high-speed, plummeting courtship dive would blow back anybody's hair, or in the case of the Horned Lark, its two unique black "horns." • This bird's tinkling song will be one of the first you hear introducing spring. Horned Larks are often abundant at roadsides, searching for seeds, but an approaching vehicle usually sends them flying into an adjacent field. During winter, you can spot large groups of these birds in farmers' fields or catch them at the beach visiting with Snow Buntings and Lapland Longspurs.

Other ID: *Male:* light yellow to white face; pale throat; dull brown upperparts. *Female:* duller plumage.
Size: *L* 7 in; *W* 12 in.
Voice: call is a tinkling *tsee-titi* or *zoot;* flight song is a long series of tinkling, twittered whistles.
Status: fairly common permanent resident.
Habitat: open areas, including pastures, native prairie, cultivated or sparsely vegetated fields, golf courses and airfields.

Similar Birds

Snow Bunting

Lapland Longspur

American Pipit

small black "horns"
(rarely raised)

black line under
eye extends from
bill to "cheek"

dark tail with
white outer tail
feathers

black breast
band

♂

Nesting: on the ground; in a shallow scrape lined with grass and plant fibers; brown-blotched, gray to greenish white eggs are 1 x ⅝ in; female incubates 3–4 eggs for 10–12 days.

Did You Know?

One way to distinguish a sparrow from a Horned Lark is by their method of travel: Horned Larks walk, whereas sparrows hop.

Look For

This bird's dark tail contrasts with its light brown body and belly. This feature will help you to spot the Horned Lark in its open-country habitat.

Purple Martin

Progne subis

These large swallows will entertain you throughout spring and summer in return for you setting up luxurious "condo complexes" for them. Martin adults spiral around their accommodations in pursuit of flying insects, while their young perch clumsily at the cavity openings. Purple Martins once nested in natural tree hollows and in cliff crevices, but they now have virtually abandoned these in favor of human-made housing. • To avoid the invasion of aggressive House Sparrows or European Starlings, it is essential for martin condos to be cleaned out and closed up after each nesting season.

Other ID: pointed wings; small bill.
Female: sooty gray underparts.
Size: L 7–8 in; W 18 in.
Voice: rich, fluty, robinlike *pew-pew*, often heard in flight.
Status: fairly common summer resident.
Habitat: semi-open areas, often near water.

Similar Birds

European Starling
(p. 142)

Barn Swallow (p. 120)

Tree Swallow

glossy, dark
blue body

slightly
forked tail

♀

dark underparts
on male

♂

Nesting: communal; in a birdhouse or hollowed-out gourd; nest is made of feathers, grass and mud; white eggs are 1 x ⅝ in; female incubates 4–5 eggs for 15–18 days.

Did You Know?

The Purple Martin is North America's largest swallow.

Look For

Purple Martins are attracted to martin condo complexes that are erected in open areas, high on a pole and near a body of water.

Northern Rough-winged Swallow

Stelgidopteryx serripennis

Small and quick, Northern Rough-winged Swallows are more widespread in Missouri than most people realize. They typically nest in sandy banks along rivers and streams, but vertical cuts created by inter-state highways have provided additional nesting crevices for these dusky little birds. Watch for Rough-wings zipping through busy intersections near banks, culverts and bridges. • Male Northern Rough-wings have unique, curved barbs along the outer edges of their primary wing feathers. The purpose of this saw-toothed edge remains a mystery, but it may be used to produce sound during courtship displays.

Other ID: light brownish gray underparts; small bill; plumage color varies considerably in populations. *In flight:* long, pointed wings; square tail.
Size: L 5½ in; W 14 in.
Voice: generally quiet; occasionally a quick, short, squeaky *brrrtt*.
Status: common summer resident.
Habitat: open and semi-open areas, including fields and open woodlands, usually near water; also gravel pits.

Similar Birds

Bank Swallow

Tree Swallow

Cliff Swallow

drab brown overall

gray-brown throat, chest and sides

Nesting: occasionally in a small colony; pair excavates a long burrow in a steep, earthen bank; may use an existing burrow; nest is lined with leaves; white eggs are $^{11}/_{16}$ x $^{1}/_{2}$ in; mostly the female incubates 4–8 eggs for 12–16 days.

Did You Know?

This bird is named for its wings: *Stelgidopteryx* means "scraper wing," and *serripennis* means "saw feather."

Look For

The Rough-wing is more likely than other swallows to feed over water, picking off insects on or near the water's surface.

Barn Swallow
Hirundo rustica

When you encounter this bird, you might first notice its distinctive, deeply forked tail—or you might just find yourself repeatedly ducking to avoid the dives of a protective parent. • Barn Swallows once nested on cliffs, but they are now found more frequently nesting on barns, boathouses and areas under bridges and house eaves. The messy young and aggressive parents unfortunately often bring people to remove nests just as nesting season is beginning, but this bird's close association with humans allows us to observe the normally secretive reproductive cycle of birds.

Other ID: blue-black upperparts; long, pointed wings.
Size: *L* 7 in; *W* 15 in.
Voice: continuous, twittering chatter: *zip-zip-zip* or *kvick-kvick*.
Status: common summer resident.
Habitat: open rural and urban areas where bridges, culverts and buildings are found near water.

Similar Birds

Cliff Swallow

Purple Martin (p. 116)

Tree Swallow

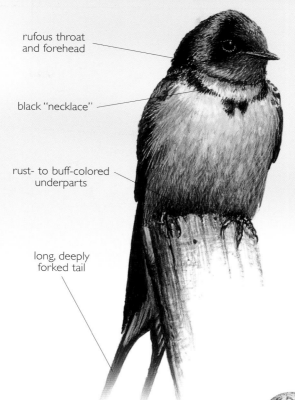

rufous throat and forehead

black "necklace"

rust- to buff-colored underparts

long, deeply forked tail

Nesting: singly or in small, loose colonies; on a human-made structure under an overhang; half or full cup nest is made of mud, grass and straw; brown-spotted, white eggs are ¾ x ½ in; pair incubates 4–7 eggs for 13–17 days.

Did You Know?

The Barn Swallow is a natural pest controller, feeding on insects that are often harmful to crops and livestock.

Look For

Barn Swallows roll mud into small balls and build their nests one mouthful of mud at a time.

Carolina Chickadee
Poecile carolinensis

Fidgety, friendly Carolina Chickadees are familiar to anyone with a backyard feeder well stocked with sunflower seeds and peanut butter. These agile birds even hang upside down to pluck up insects and berries. Carolina Chickadees will hoard food for later in the season when food may become scarce.
• A chickadee uses its tiny bill to excavate a nesting cavity. Come breeding season, this energetic little bird can be found hammering out a hollow in a rotting tree. • The Carolina Chickadee is most common in southern Missouri, whereas the Black-capped Chickadee *(P. atricapillus)* predominates in the north. Their ranges overlap in the Glaciated and Osage plains.

Other ID: white "cheeks"; white underparts; buffy flanks.
Size: L 4¾ in; W 7½ in.
Voice: whistling song has 4 clear notes: *fee-bee fee-bay.*
Status: common permanent resident in southern Missouri.
Habitat: deciduous and mixed woods, riparian woodlands, groves and isolated shade trees; frequents urban areas.

Similar Birds

Black-capped Chickadee

White-breasted Nuthatch (p. 126)

Blackpoll Warbler

black cap and "bib"

grayish nape

gray upperparts
and secondaries

Nesting: excavates or enlarges a tree cavity; may also use a nest box; cavity is lined with soft material; white eggs, marked with reddish brown are $9/16$ x $7/16$ in; female incubates 5–8 eggs for 11–14 days.

Did You Know?

Each fall, adult Carolina Chickadees tour the neighborhood, introducing their offspring to the best feeding spots.

Look For

Alert Carolina Chickadees are often the first to issue alarm calls, warning other birds that danger is near.

Tufted Titmouse
Baeolophus bicolor

This bird's amusing feeding antics and its insatiable appetite keep curious observers entertained at bird feeders. Grasping a sunflower seed with its tiny feet, the dexterous Tufted Titmouse will strike its dainty bill repeatedly against the hard outer coating to expose the inner core. • A breeding pair of Tufted Titmice will maintain their bond throughout the year, even when joining small, mixed flocks for the cold winter months. The titmouse family bond is so strong that the young from one breeding season will often stay with their parents long enough to help them with nesting and feeding duties the following year.

Other ID: white underparts; pale face.
Size: *L* 6–6½ in; *W* 10 in.
Voice: noisy, scolding call, like that of a chickadee; song is a whistled *peter peter* or *peter peter peter*.
Status: common permanent resident.
Habitat: deciduous woodlands, groves and suburban parks with large, mature trees.

Look For

Easily identified by its gray crest and upperparts and black forehead, the Tufted Titmouse can often be seen at feeders. Studies have shown that titmice always choose the largest sunflower seeds available to them, and during winter, they often cache food in bark crevices.

gray crest

black forehead

gray upperparts

buffy flanks

Nesting: in a natural cavity or woodpecker cavity lined with soft vegetation, moss and animal hair; heavily spotted, white eggs are $^{11}/_{16}$ x $^{9}/_{16}$ in; female incubates 5–6 eggs for 12–14 days.

Did You Know?

Nesting pairs search for soft nest-lining material in late winter and may accept an offering of the hair that has accumulated in your hairbrush.

White-breasted Nuthatch

Sitta carolinensis

Its upside-down antics and noisy, nasal call make the White-breasted Nuthatch a favorite among novice birders. Whether you spot this black-capped bullet spiraling headfirst down a tree or clinging to the underside of a branch in search of invertebrates, the nuthatch's odd behavior deserves a second glance. • Comparing the White-breasted Nuthatch to the Carolina Chickadee, both regular visitors to backyard feeders, is a perfect starting point for introductory birding. Although both species have dark crowns and gray backs, the nuthatch's foraging behaviors and undulating flight pattern are distinctive.

Other ID: white underparts and face; straight bill; short legs.
Size: L 5½–6 in; W 11 in.
Voice: song is a fast, nasal *yank-hank yank-hank*, lower than the Red-breasted Nuthatch; calls include *ha-ha-ha ha-ha-ha, ank ank* and *ip*.
Status: common permanent resident.
Habitat: mixedwood forests, woodlots and backyards.

Similar Birds

Red-breasted Nuthatch   Carolina Chickadee (p. 122)   Brown Creeper

rusty undertail coverts

gray-blue back

dark gray cap

♀

short tail

♂

black cap

Nesting: in a natural cavity or abandoned woodpecker nest; female lines the cavity with soft material; brown-speckled, white eggs are ¾ x ⁹/₁₆ in; female incubates 5–8 eggs for 12–14 days.

Did You Know?

Nuthatches are presumably named for their habit of wedging seeds and nuts into crevices and hacking them open with their bills.

Look For

Nuthatches grasp the tree through foot power alone, unlike woodpeckers, which use their tails to brace themselves against tree trunks.

Carolina Wren
Thryothorus ludovicianus

The energetic and cheerful Carolina Wren can be shy and retiring, often hiding deep inside dense shrubbery. The best opportunity for viewing this particularly vocal wren is when it sits on a conspicuous perch while unleashing its impressive song. Pairs perform lively "duets" at any time of day and in any season. The duet often begins with introductory chatter by the female, followed by innumerable ringing variations of *tea-kettle tea-kettle tea-kettle tea* from her mate. • Carolina Wrens readily nest in the brushy thickets of an overgrown backyard or in an obscure nook or crevice in a house or barn. If conditions are favorable, two broods may be raised in a single season.

Other ID: white throat; slightly downcurved bill.
Size: L 5½ in; W 7½ in.
Voice: loud, repetitious *tea-kettle tea-kettle tea-kettle* may be heard at any time of day or year; female often chatters while male sings.
Status: common permanent resident.
Habitat: dense forest undergrowth, especially shrubby tangles and thickets.

Similar Birds

House Wren

Winter Wren

Red-breasted Nuthatch

rusty brown
upperparts

long, prominent,
white "eyebrow"

rich buff-colored
underparts

Nesting: in a nest box or natural or artificial cavity; nest is lined with soft material, including snakeskin at entrance; brown-blotched, white eggs are ¾ x ⁹⁄₁₆ in; female incubates 4–5 eggs for 12–16 days.

Did You Know?

In mild winters, Carolina Wren populations remain stable, but frigid temperatures can temporarily decimate an otherwise healthy population.

Look For

A nesting Carolina Wren will not hesitate to give intruders a severe scolding but will remain hidden all the while.

Eastern Bluebird
Sialia sialis

The Eastern Bluebird's enticing colors are like those of a warm setting sun against a deep blue sky. • This cavity nester's survival has been put to the test in the past—populations have declined in the presence of the competitive, introduced House Sparrow and European Starling. The removal of standing dead trees has also diminished nest site availability. Thankfully, bluebird enthusiasts and organizations have developed "bluebird trails" and mounted nest boxes on fence posts along highways and rural roads, allowing Eastern Bluebird numbers to gradually recover.

Other ID: dark bill and legs. *Female:* thin, white eye ring; gray-brown head and back tinged with blue; blue wings and tail; paler chestnut underparts.
Size: L 7 in; W 13 in.
Voice: song is a rich, warbling *turr, turr-lee, turr-lee;* call is a chittering *pew.*
Status: fairly common permanent resident.
Habitat: cropland fencelines, meadows, fallow and abandoned fields, pastures, forest clearings and edges, golf courses, large lawns and cemeteries.

Similar Birds

Blue Grosbeak (p. 168)   Indigo Bunting (p. 170)

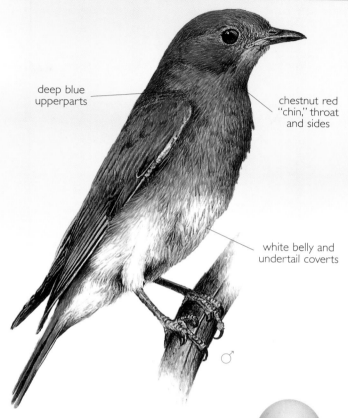

deep blue
upperparts

chestnut red
"chin," throat
and sides

white belly and
undertail coverts

♂

Nesting: in a natural cavity or nest box; female
builds a cup nest of grass, weed stems and small
twigs; pale blue eggs are ⅞ x ⅝ in; female
incubates 4–5 eggs for 13–16 days.

Did You Know?

A cold spell in spring can
kill the Eastern Bluebird,
freezing the eggs and adult
while it sits on the nest.

Look For

The Eastern Bluebird uses an
elevated perch as a base
from which to hunt insects.
They also feed on berries,
especially wild grapes, sumac
and currents.

Wood Thrush
Hylocichla mustelina

The loud, warbled notes of the Wood Thrush once resounded through our woodlands, but forest fragmentation and urban sprawl have eliminated much of this bird's nesting habitat. Broken forests and diminutive woodlots have allowed for the invasion of common, open-area predators and parasites, such as raccoons, skunks, crows, jays and cowbirds. Traditionally, these predators had little access to nests that were hidden deep within vast hardwood forests. Many forests that have been urbanized or developed for agriculture now host families of American Robins rather than the once-prominent Wood Thrushes.

Other ID: plump body; streaked "cheeks"; brown wings, rump and tail.
Size: *L* 8 in; *W* 13 in.
Voice: *Male:* bell-like phrases of 3–5 notes, with each note at a different pitch and followed by a trill: *Will you live with me? Way up high in a tree, I'll come right down and…seeee!;* calls include a *pit pit* and *bweebeebeep.*
Status: fairly common summer resident.
Habitat: moist, mature and preferably undisturbed deciduous woodlands and mixed forests.

Similar Birds

American Robin
(p. 134)

Swainson's Thrush

Veery

rusty head
and back

bold, white
eye ring

large, black spots
on white breast,
sides and flanks

Nesting: low in a fork of a deciduous tree; female builds a bulky cup nest of vegetation held together with mud and lined with softer material; pale greenish blue eggs are 1 x ¾ in; female incubates 3–4 eggs for 13–14 days.

Did You Know?

Henry David Thoreau considered the Wood Thrush's song to be the most beautiful of avian sounds. The male can even sing two notes at once!

Look For

Wood Thrushes forage on the ground or glean vegetation for insects and other invertebrates.

American Robin

Turdus migratorius

Come March, the familiar song of the American Robin may wake you early if you are a light sleeper. This abundant bird adapts easily to urban areas and often works from dawn until after dusk when there is a nest to be built or hungry young mouths to feed. • The robin's bright red belly contrasts with its dark head and wings, making the robin easy to identify. • In winter, fruit trees may attract flocks of robins, which gather to drink the fermenting fruit's intoxicating juices.

Other ID: incomplete, white eye ring; gray-brown back; white undertail coverts.
Size: *L* 10 in; *W* 17 in.
Voice: song is an evenly spaced warble: *cheerily cheer-up cheerio;* call is a rapid *tut-tut-tut.*
Status: abundant permanent resident.
Habitat: *Breeding:* residential lawns and gardens, pastures, urban parks, broken forests, bogs and river shorelines. *Winter:* near fruit-bearing trees and springs.

Similar Birds

Veery

Look For

A hunting robin with its head tilted to the side isn't listening for prey—it is actually looking for movements in the soil.

black head

dark gray head

black-tipped, yellow bill

brick red breast is darker on male

white throat is streaked with black

♂   ♀

Nesting: in a tree or shrub; cup nest is built of grass, moss, bark and mud; light blue eggs are 1⅛ x ¾ in; female incubates 4 eggs for 11–16 days; raises up to 3 broods per year.

Did You Know?

American Robins do not use nest boxes; they prefer platforms for their nests. Robins usually raise two broods per year, and the male cares for the fledglings from the first brood while the female incubates the second clutch of eggs.

Gray Catbird

Dumetella carolinensis

This accomplished mimic may fool you
if you hear it shuffling through underbrush
and dense riparian shrubs, calling its catlike
meow. Its mimicking talents are further enhanced
by its ability to sing two notes at once, using each
side of its syrinx individually. • The Gray Catbird
will vigilantly defend its territory against sparrows,
robins, cowbirds and other intruders. It will
destroy the eggs and nestlings of other songbirds
and will take on an intense defensive posture if
approached, screaming and even attempting to hit
an intruder.

Other ID: dark gray overall; black eyes, bill and legs.
Size: *L* 8½–9 in; *W* 11 in.
Voice: calls include a catlike *meow* and a harsh *check-
check*; song is a variety of warbles, squeaks
and mimicked phrases interspersed with a
mew call.
Status: common summer resident in northern Missouri; less common in the south.
Habitat: dense thickets, brambles, shrubby or
brushy areas and hedgerows, often near water.

Similar Birds

Northern Mockingbird
(p. 138)

Look For

If you catch a glimpse of this
bird during breeding season,
watch the male raise his long
slender tail into the air to
show off his rust-colored
undertail coverts.

black cap

long, dark gray
to black tail

chestnut undertail
coverts

Nesting: in a dense shrub or thicket; bulky cup nest is made of twigs, leaves and grass; greenish blue eggs are ⅞ x ⅝ in; female incubates 4 eggs for 12–15 days.

Did You Know?

The watchful female Gray Catbird can recognize a Brown-headed Cowbird egg and will remove it from her nest. The ability to recognize the foreign eggs is learned, and only about a dozen species are able to do so.

Northern Mockingbird

Mimus polyglottos

Northern Mockingbirds have an amazing vocal repertoire that includes over 400 different song types, which they belt out incessantly during breeding season, serenading throughout the night during a full moon. • A mockingbird can imitate almost anything. In fact, this bird can replicate some sounds so accurately that even computerized auditory analysis is unable to detect the difference between the original sound and the mockingbird's imitation.

Other ID: gray upperparts; pale gray underparts.
In flight: large, white patch at base of black primaries
Size: *L* 10 in; *W* 14 in.
Voice: song is a medley of mimicked phrases, with the phrases often repeated 3–6 times; calls include a harsh *chair* and *chewk*.
Status: common permanent resident.
Habitat: hedges, suburban gardens and orchard margins with an abundance of available fruit; hedgerows of roses are especially important in winter.
Nesting: often in a small shrub or small tree;

Similar Birds

Loggerhead Shrike

Gray Catbird (p. 136)

long, dark tail with white outer tail feathers

thin, dark eye line

dark wings with 2 thin, white wing bars

cup nest is built with twigs and plants; brown-blotched, bluish gray to greenish eggs are 1 x ⅝ in; female incubates 3–4 eggs for 12–13 days.

Did You Know?

The scientific name *poly-glottos* is Greek for "many tongues" and refers to this bird's ability to mimic a wide variety of sounds.

Look For

The Northern Mockingbird's energetic territorial dance is delightful to watch as males square off in what appears to be a swordless fencing duel.

Brown Thrasher
Toxostoma rufum

The Brown Thrasher shares the streaked breast of a thrush and the long tail of a catbird, but it has a temper all its own. Because it nests close to the ground, the Brown Thrasher defends its nest with a vengeance, attacking snakes and other nest robbers, sometimes to the point of drawing blood. • Biologists have estimated that the male Brown Thrasher is capable of producing up to 3000 distinctive song phrases—the most extensive vocal repertoire of any North American bird.

Other ID: reddish brown upperparts; long, rufous tail; yellow-orange eyes.
Size: *L* 11½ in; *W* 13 in.
Voice: sings a large variety of phrases, with each phrase usually repeated twice: *dig-it dig-it, hoe-it hoe-it, pull-it-up pull-it-up;* calls include a loud crackling note, a harsh *shuck,* a soft *churr* and a whistled, 3-note *pit-cher-ee.*
Status: common summer resident; uncommon winter resident.
Habitat: dense shrubs and thickets, overgrown pastures, woodland edges and brushy areas, rarely close to urban areas.

Similar Birds

Hermit Thrush   Wood Thrush (p. 132)

long, downcurved bill

gray "cheek"

2 white wing bars

pale underparts with heavy brown streaking

Nesting: usually in a low shrub; often on the ground; cup nest made of grass, twigs and leaves is lined with fine vegetation; brown-spotted, pale blue eggs are 1 x ¾ in; pair incubates 4 eggs for 11–14 days.

Did You Know?

Fencing patches of shrubs and wooded areas bordering wetlands and streams can prevent cattle from devastating thrasher nesting habitat.

Look For

The Brown Thrasher can be hard to find in its shrubby understory habitat. You might catch only a flash of rufous as it flies from one thicket to another.

European Starling

Sturnus vulgaris

The European Starling did not hesitate to make itself known across North America after being released in New York's Central Park in 1890 and 1891. This highly adaptable bird not only took over the nest sites of native cavity nesters, such as Tree Swallows and Red-headed Woodpeckers, but it also learned to mimic the sounds of Killdeers, Red-tailed Hawks, Soras and meadowlarks. • Look for European Starlings in massive evening roosts under bridges or on buildings from late summer through winter.

Other ID: dark eyes; short, squared tail.
Nonbreeding: feather tips are heavily spotted with white and buff.
Size: *L* 8½ in; *W* 16 in.
Voice: variety of whistles, squeaks, and gurgles; imitates other birds.
Status: abundant permanent resident.
Habitat: cities, towns, residential areas, farmyards, woodland fringes and clearings.

Similar Birds

Rusty Blackbird

Brewer's Blackbird

Brown-headed Cowbird (p. 176)

iridescent, purple-black
head, neck and breast

glossy, green back
with buffy spots

yellow bill

greenish black
underparts

breeding

Nesting: in an abandoned woodpecker cavity, natural cavity or nest box; nest is made of grass, twigs and straw; bluish to greenish white eggs are 1⅛ x ⅞ in; female incubates 4–6 eggs for 12–14 days.

Did You Know?

This bird was brought to New York as part of the local Shakespeare society's plan to introduce all the birds mentioned in their favorite author's writings.

Look For

Sometimes confused with a blackbird, the European Starling has a shorter tail and a bright yellow bill.

Cedar Waxwing

Bombycilla cedrorum

With its black "mask" and slick hairdo, the Cedar Waxwing has a heroic look. This bird's splendid personality is reflected in its amusing antics after it gorges on fermented berries and in its gentle courtship dance. To court a mate, the gentlemanly male hops toward a female and offers her a berry. The female accepts the berry and hops away, then stops and hops back toward the male to offer him the berry in return. • If a bird's crop is full and it can't eat any more, it will continue to pluck fruit and pass it down the line like a bucket brigade, until the fruit is gulped down by a still-hungry bird.

Other ID: brown upperparts; yellow wash on belly; gray rump; yellow terminal tail band.
Size: *L* 7 in; *W* 12 in.
Voice: faint, high-pitched, trilled whistle: *tseee-tseee-tseee.*
Status: fairly common permanent resident locally; more common in migration.
Habitat: wooded residential parks and gardens, overgrown fields, forest edges, second-growth, riparian and open woodlands; often near fruit trees and water.

Similar Birds

Bohemian Waxwing

Look For

The yellow tail band and "waxy" red wing tips of the Cedar Waxwing get their color from pigments in the berries that this bird eats.

cinnamon crest

black "mask"

small red "drops" on wings

white undertail coverts

Nesting: in a tree or shrub; cup nest is made of twigs, moss and lichen; darkly spotted, bluish to gray eggs are $\frac{7}{8}$ x $\frac{5}{8}$ in; female incubates 3–5 eggs for 12–16 days.

Did You Know?

The Bohemian Waxwing is a casual winter resident and is seen only occasionally in Missouri. It has brown undertail coverts, whereas those of the Cedar Waxwing are white.

Northern Parula

Parula americana

The small, colorful Northern Parula is a summer forest resident that prefers open woodlands, especially near water. Young Northern Parulas spend the first few weeks of their lives enclosed in a fragile, basketlike nest suspended from a tree branch. Once they have grown too large for the nest and their wing feathers are strong enough to allow for a short, awkward flight, the young leave their warm abode, dispersing them-selves among nearby trees and shrubs. • As warm summer nights slip away to be replaced by cooler fall temperatures, Northern Parulas migrate to the warmer climes of Central America.

Other ID: 2 bold, white wing bars; white belly and flanks.
Size: L 4½ in; W 7 in.
Voice: song is a rising, buzzy trill ending with an abrupt lower *zip*.
Status: common summer resident in the south; less common in the north.
Habitat: *Breeding:* moist coniferous forests, humid riparian woodlands and swampy deciduous woodlands, especially with hanging lichens. *In migration:* woodlands or areas with tall shrubs.

Similar Birds

Cerulean Warbler

Blue-winged Warbler

Yellow-rumped Warbler

Yellow-throated Warbler

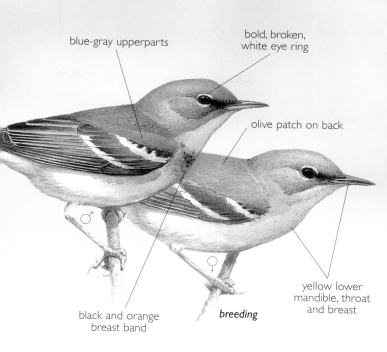

blue-gray upperparts

bold, broken, white eye ring

olive patch on back

♂

♀

yellow lower mandible, throat and breast

black and orange breast band

breeding

Nesting: usually in a conifer; small hanging nest is woven by the female into hanging strands of tree lichens; may add lichens to a dense cluster of conifer boughs; brown-marked, whitish eggs are ⅝ x ½ in; pair incubates 4–5 eggs for 12–14 days.

Did You Know?

In spring, Northern Parulas are among the earliest warblers to return to breed in our state.

Look For

Males often sing among the tops of tall coniferous spires, where they are often fearless and easily approached.

American Redstart

Setophaga ruticilla

Known as "Butterfly Bird" in some parts of its range, the American Redstart rarely, if ever, sits still. Its Latin American name, *candelita*, meaning "little torch," also describes it perfectly. Not only are the male's bright orange patches the color of a glowing flame, but the bird never ceases to flicker, even when perched. • In its seemingly nonstop pursuit of prey, the American Redstart flushes insects with the flash of color from its wings or tail. Then it uses its broad bill and rictal bristles (the short, whiskerlike feathers around its mouth) to capture insects like an expert flycatcher.

Other ID: *Male:* white belly and undertail coverts. *Female:* white underparts.
Size: L 5 in; W 8½ in.
Voice: male's song is a highly variable series of *tseet* or *zee* notes at different pitches; call is a sharp, sweet *chip*.
Status: fairly common locally in summer.
Habitat: shrubby woodland edges; open and semi-open forests with a regenerating deciduous understory; often near water; prefers alder swales and thickets in migration.

Similar Birds

Baltimore Oriole

Orchard Oriole
(p. 178)

olive brown
upperparts

yellow foreshoulder,
wing and tail patches

black head and
upperparts

♀

♂

red-orange shoulder,
wing and tail patches

Nesting: in a shrub or sapling; female builds open cup nest of plant down, bark shreds, grass and rootlets; brown-marked, whitish eggs are ⅝ x ½ in; female incubates 4 eggs for 11–12 days.

Did You Know?

This bird's high-pitched, lisping, trilly songs are so variable that identifying an American Redstart by song alone is a challenge for birders of all levels.

Look For

Even when an American Redstart is perched, its color-splashed tail sways rhythmically back and forth.

Louisiana Waterthrush
Seiurus motacilla

The Louisiana Waterthrush is often seen along the shorelines of babbling streams in search of its next meal. Usually found near swamps and sluggish waterways, it only inhabit shorelines of fast-flowing waterways where its range overlaps with the Northern Waterthrush *(S. noveboracensis)*.

• The Louisiana Waterthrush has whiter underparts, bright pink legs, a broad, white eye stripe that does not taper behind the eye and less streaking on its throat than the Northern Waterthrush. Both waterthrushes bob their heads and move their tails up and down as they walk, but the Louisiana Waterthrush bobs its tail more slowly and also tends to sway from side to side.

Other ID: brownish upperparts; long bill.
Size: L 6 in; W 10 in.
Voice: song begins with 3–4 distinctive, shrill, slurred notes followed by a warbling twitter; call is a brisk *chick* or *chink*.
Status: common summer resident in southern Missouri; uncommon in the north.
Habitat: moist, forested ravines, alongside fast-flowing streams; rarely along wooded swamps.

Similar Birds

Northern Waterthrush

Ovenbird

Wood Thrush (p. 132)

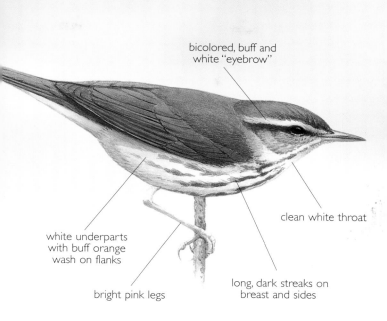

bicolored, buff and white "eyebrow"

clean white throat

white underparts with buff orange wash on flanks

bright pink legs

long, dark streaks on breast and sides

Nesting: concealed within a rocky hollow or tangled tree roots; cup nest of vegetation is lined with animal hair, ferns and rootlets; creamy white, spotted eggs are ¾ x ⁹⁄₁₆ in; female incubates 3–6 eggs for about 14 days.

Did You Know?

This bird's genus name, *Seiurus*, and its species name, *motacilla*, both mean "tail waver" referring to its tail-wagging habit.

Look For

Similar-looking Northern Waterthrushes can be seen in our state during spring and fall migration.

Common Yellowthroat

Geothlypis trichas

The bumblebee colors of the male Common Yellowthroat's black "mask" and yellow throat identify this skulking wetland resident. The cattail outposts from which he perches to sing his *witchety* song are strategically chosen, and he visits them in rotation, fiercely guarding his territory against the intrusion of other males. • The Common Yellowthroat is different from most wood-warblers, preferring marshlands and wet, overgrown meadows to forests. • The female wears no "mask" and remains mostly hidden from view in thick vegetation when she tends to the nest.

Other ID: black bill; orangy legs. *Female:* may show faint, white eye ring.
Size: *L* 5 in; *W* 7 in.
Voice: song is a clear, oscillating *witchety witchety witchety-witch;* call is a sharp *tcheck* or *tchet.*
Status: abundant summer resident.
Habitat: coastal areas; wetlands, riparian areas and wet, overgrown meadows; sometimes dry fields.

Similar Birds

Wilson's Warbler   Nashville Warbler

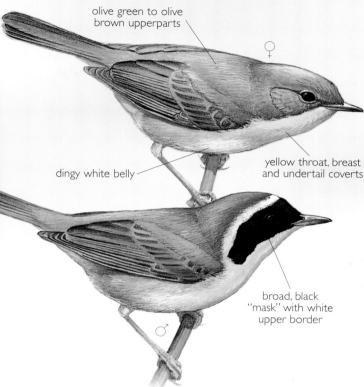

olive green to olive brown upperparts

♀

dingy white belly

yellow throat, breast and undertail coverts

broad, black "mask" with white upper border

♂

Nesting: on or near the ground or in a small shrub or emergent vegetation; female builds an open cup nest of weeds, grass, bark strips and moss; brown-blotched, white eggs are ⅝ × ½ in; female incubates 3–5 eggs for 12 days.

Did You Know?

Famous Swedish biologist Carl Linnaeus named the Common Yellowthroat in 1766, making it one of the first North American birds to be described.

Look For

Common Yellowthroats immerse themselves or roll in water, then shake off the excess water by flicking or flapping their wings.

Yellow-breasted Chat

Icteria virens

Nearly 8 inches in length, the Yellow-breasted Chat is quite literally a "warbler and a half." This bird is a member of the wood-warbler clan, and its bright yellow coloration and intense curiosity are typical warbler traits. However, the chat's large size, curious vocalizations and noisy thrashing behavior suggest a close relationship to the mimic thrushes. • When much of eastern North America was logged in the early 1900s, the Yellow-breasted Chat became one of our most common breeding birds. Populations have since declined as woodlands mature and shrubby riparian habitat are lost to development.

Other ID: white jaw line; heavy, black bill; olive-green upperparts; gray-black legs. *Male:* black lores. *Female:* gray lores.
Size: L 7½ in; W 9¾ in.
Voice: single notes or phrases of slurred piping whistles, *kuks*, harsh rattles and "laughs"; persistent night singing in spring.
Status: common summer resident.
Habitat: dense riparian thickets bordering streams, small ponds and swampy ground; in some situations breeds in extensive hillside bramble patches.

Look For

Often heard but difficult to see, this elusive bird avoids detection by skulking through brushy riparian thickets and tangled fencerows. The male is most vocal early in the breeding season.

white "spectacles"

black lores

yellow breast

white undertail
coverts

long tail

♂

Nesting: low in a shrub or a small tree; well-concealed, bulky nest is made of leaves, straw and weeds, with a tight inner cup woven with bark and plant fibers; brown-speckled, creamy white eggs are $7/8$ x $5/8$ in; female incubates 3–4 eggs for about 11 days.

Did You Know?

Yellow-breasted Chats are well known for singing at night during spring. Only the males sing and they have a repertoire of highly variable songs. On average a male chat may sing 60 different songs.

Summer Tanager
Piranga rubra

The Summer Tanager is a treat for southern birders—most of North America only gets a glimpse of these beauties if a rare individual flies off track. These striking birds breed throughout our forested areas, favoring the edges of pine or pine-oak forests and riparian areas. • Summer Tanagers thrive on a wide variety of insects, but are best known for snatching flying bees and wasps from menacing swarms. They may even harass the occupants of a wasp nest until the nest is abandoned and the larvae inside are left free for the picking.

Other ID: *Immature male:* patchy, red and greenish plumage.
Size: *L* 7–8 in; *W* 12 in.
Voice: song is a series of 3–5 sweet, clear, whistled phrases, like a faster version of the American Robin's song; call is *pit* or *pit-a-tuck.*
Status: common in southern Missouri in summer.
Habitat: mixed coniferous and deciduous woodlands, especially those with oak or hickory, or riparian woodlands with cottonwoods; occasionally in wooded backyards.

Similar Birds

Scarlet Tanager

Northern Cardinal
(p. 164)

Orchard Oriole
(p. 178)

thick, pale bill

varies from overall grayish yellow to greenish with reddish wash

small crest

rose red overall

Nesting: on a high, horizontal tree limb; female builds a flimsy, shallow cup of grass, Spanish moss and twigs and lines it with fine grass; brown-spotted, pale blue-green eggs are ⅞ x ⅝ in; female incubates 3–4 eggs for 11–12 days.

Did You Know?

The male Summer Tanager keeps his rosy red plumage all year, unlike the male Scarlet Tanager, which temporarily molts to a greenish yellow plumage in fall.

Look For

A courting male tanager will hop persistently in front of or over the female while offering her food and fanning his handsome crest and tail feathers.

Eastern Towhee
Pipilo erythrophthalmus

Eastern Towhees are large, colorful members of the sparrow family. These noisy birds are often heard before they are seen as they rustle about in dense undergrowth, craftily scraping back layers of dry leaves to expose the seeds, berries or insects hidden beneath. They employ an unusual two-footed technique to uncover food items—a strategy that is especially important in winter when very little food is left on the ground. • The Eastern Towhee and its western relative, the Spotted Towhee *(P. maculatus),* were once grouped together as the "Rufous-sided Towhee."

Other ID: white outer tail corners, lower breast and belly; buff undertail coverts; eyes commonly red, but in southeastern U.S. may be white or orange.
Size: L 7–8½ in; W 10½ in.
Voice: song is 2 high, whistled notes followed by a trill: *drink your teeeee;* call is a scratchy, slurred *cheweee!* or *chewink!*
Status: abundant summer resident; uncommon winter resident.
Habitat: along woodland edges; in shrubby, abandoned fields and residential areas.

Similar Birds

Dark-eyed Junco
(p. 162)

Look For

Showy towhees are easily attracted to feeders, where they scratch on the ground for millet, oats or sunflower seeds.

black back, "hood" and bill

brown "hood" and upperparts.

♂

rufous sides and flanks

♀

small, white wing patch

Nesting: on the ground or low in a dense shrub; female builds a cup nest of twigs, bark strips, grass and animal hair; brown-spotted, creamy white eggs are $7/8 \times 5/8$ in; mainly the female incubates 3–4 eggs for 12–13 days.

Did You Know?

The scientific name *erythrophthalmus* means "red eye" in Greek, though towhees in the southeastern states may have white or orange irises.

Field Sparrow

Spizella pusilla

A plaintive whistle issued from an overgrown field, pasture or forest clearing can signal the Field Sparrow's presence. This gentle bird breeds throughout our state, concealing a delicate nest near the ground, among bushes or in clumps of tall grass.

• Over time, the Field Sparrow has learned to recognize when its nest has been parasitized by the Brown-headed Cowbird. Because the unwelcome eggs are usually too large for this small sparrow to eject, the nest is simply abandoned. Field Sparrows may make numerous nesting attempts in a single season.

Other ID: gray face and throat; pinkish legs. *Rufous morph:* rusty streak behind eye; buffy red wash on breast, sides and flanks.

Size: *L* 5–6 in; *W* 8 in.

Voice: song is a series of woeful, musical, down-slurred whistles accelerating into a trill; call is a *chip* or *tsee*.

Status: common summer resident; uncommon in winter.

Habitat: abandoned or weedy and overgrown fields and pastures, woodland edges and clearings, extensive shrubby riparian areas and young conifer plantations.

Similar Birds

Chipping Sparrow   American Tree Sparrow

rusty crown with gray central stripe

white eye ring

2 white wings bars

large, orange-pink bill

long tail

unmarked, gray or buffy underparts

Nesting: on or near the ground, often sheltered by a shrub; female weaves an open cup nest of grass and lines it with soft material; brown-spotted, whitish to pale bluish eggs are $^{11}/_{16}$ x $^{1}/_{2}$ in; female incubates 3–5 eggs for 10–12 days.

Did You Know?

In fall, hundreds of Field Sparrows may crowd into weedy fields to feed.

Look For

Its pink bill and rusty crown help to distinguish the Field Sparrow from other similar small brown birds.

Dark-eyed Junco

Junco hyemalis

Juncos usually congregate in backyards with bird feeders and sheltering conifers—with such amenities at their disposal, more and more juncos are appearing in urban areas. Juncos spend most of their time on the ground, snatching up seeds underneath bird feeders, and they are readily flushed from wooded trails and backyard feeders. Their distinctive, white outer tail feathers flash in alarm as they seek cover in a nearby tree or shrub. • The junco is often called the "Snow Bird," and the species name *hyemalis* means "winter" in Greek.

Other ID: *Female:* gray-brown where male is slate gray.
Size: L 6–7 in; W 9 in.
Voice: song is a long, dry trill; call is a smacking *chip* note, often given in series.
Status: common winter resident throughout the state.
Habitat: shrubby woodland borders, backyard feeders.

Similar Birds

Eastern Towhee
(p. 158)

Look For

This bird will flash its distinctive white outer tail feathers as it rushes for cover after being flushed.

dark slate gray overall

pale pink bill

white outer tail feathers

white belly and undertail coverts

♂

"Slate-colored Junco"

Nesting: on the ground, usually concealed; female builds a cup nest of twigs, grass, bark shreds and moss; brown-marked, whitish to bluish eggs are ¾ x ½ in; female incubates 3–5 eggs for 12–13 days.

Did You Know?

There are five closely related Dark-eyed Junco subspecies in North America that share similar habits but differ in coloration and range.

Northern Cardinal
Cardinalis cardinalis

A male Northern Cardinal will display his unforgettable, vibrant red head crest and raise his tail when
he is excited or agitated. This colorful year-round
resident will vigorously defend his territory, even
attacking his own reflection in a window or
hubcap! • Cardinals are one of only a few bird
species to maintain strong pair bonds. Some cou-
ples sing to each other year-round, whereas others
join loose flocks, reestablishing pair bonds in spring
during a "courtship feeding." A male offers a seed to
the female, which she then accepts and eats.

Other ID: *Male:* red overall. *Female:* brownish
buff overall; fainter "mask"; red crest, wings and tail.
Size: L 8–9 in; W 12 in.
Voice: call is a metallic *chip;* song is series
of clear, bubbly whistled notes: *What cheer!
What cheer! birdie-birdie-birdie what cheer!*
Status: common permanent resident.
Habitat: brushy thickets and shrubby tangles
along forest and woodland edges; backyards
and urban and suburban parks.

Similar Birds

Summer Tanager
(p. 156)

Scarlet Tanager

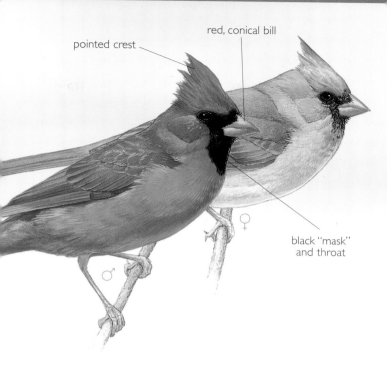

pointed crest

red, conical bill

♀

♂

black "mask"
and throat

Nesting: in a dense shrub, vine tangle or low in a coniferous tree; female builds an open cup nest of twigs, grass and bark shreds; brown-speckled, white to greenish white eggs are 1 x ¾ in; female incubates 3–4 eggs for 12–13 days.

Did You Know?

This bird owes its name to the vivid red plumage of the male, which resembles the robes of Roman Catholic cardinals.

Look For

Northern Cardinals fly with jerky movements and short glides and have a preference for sunflower seeds.

Rose-breasted Grosbeak

Pheucticus ludovicianus

Whistling its unhurried tune, the Rose-breasted Grosbeak sounds like a robin that has taken singing lessons. Although the female lacks the magnificent colors of the male, she shares his talent for beautiful song. • Mating grosbeaks often touch bills during courtship and after absences. • Rose-breasted Grosbeaks usually build their nests low in a tree or tall shrub. By contrast, they typically forage high in the canopy where they can be difficult to spot. Luckily for birders, the abundance of berries in fall often draws these birds to ground level.

Other ID: dark tail. *Male:* white underparts and rump. *Female:* thin crown stripe; brown upperparts; buff underparts with dark brown streaking.
Size: L 7–8½ in; W 12½ in.
Voice: song is a long, melodious series of whistled notes, much like a fast version of a robin's song; call is a distinctive squeak.
Status: fairly common in northern Missouri in summer.
Habitat: deciduous and mixed forests.

Similar Birds

female Purple Finch

Look For

Grosbeaks have large, pale bills that distinguish them from sparrows, which have smaller, conical bills.

bold, whitish
"eyebrow"

pale, conical bill

black "hood"
and back

♀

breeding

dark wings with small
white patches

red breast
and inner
underwings

♂

Nesting: fairly low in a tree or tall shrub, often
near water; mostly the female builds a flimsy cup
nest of plant material, lined with rootlets and hair;
brown-speckled, greenish blue eggs are 1 x 11/16 in;
pair incubates 3–5 eggs for 13–14 days.

Did You Know?

The species name *ludovicianus*, Latin for "from Louisiana," is
misleading because this bird is only a migrant through
Louisiana and other southern states.

Blue Grosbeak

Passerina caerulea

Male Blue Grosbeaks owe their spectacular spring plumage not to a fresh molt but, oddly enough, to feather wear. While Blue Grosbeaks are wintering in Mexico or Central America, their brown feather tips slowly wear away, leaving the crystal blue plumage that is seen as they arrive on their breeding grounds. The lovely blue color of the plumage is not produced by pigmentation but by tiny particles in the feathers that reflect only short wavelengths in the light spectrum. Watch for these birds perched on electrical wires, searching for their next meal. • In spring, look for the tail-spreading, tail-flicking and crown-raising behaviors that suggest the birds might be breeding.

Other ID: *Male:* black around base of bill. *Female:* whitish throat; rump and shoulders are faintly washed with blue.
Size: L 6–7½ in; W 11 in.
Voice: sweet, melodious, warbling song with phrases that rise and fall; call is a loud *chink*.
Status: fairly common summer resident in southern Missouri; less common in the north.
Habitat: thick brush, riparian thickets, shrubby areas and dense weedy fields near water.

Similar Birds

Indigo Bunting (p. 170)

Look For

A pair of rusty wing bars, visible even on first-winter birds, distinguish the Blue Grosbeak from the similar-looking and much more common Indigo Bunting.

2 rusty wing bars

blue overall

♂

stubby, pale grayish,
conical bill

♀

long tail

soft brown
plumage overall

Nesting: in a shrub or low tree; cup nest is
woven with twigs, roots and grass and lined with
finer material, including paper and occasionally
shed reptile skins; pale blue eggs are $7/8$ x $5/8$ in;
female incubates 2–5 eggs for 11–12 days.

Did You Know?

Caerulea is from the Latin for "blue," a description that just
doesn't express this bird's true beauty. At a distance, the
male's striking blue plumage may look blackish.

Indigo Bunting
Passerina cyanea

The vivid electric blue male Indigo Bunting is one of the most spectacular birds in Missouri. It arrives in April or May and favors raspberry thickets as nest sites. Dense, thorny stems keep most predators at a distance, and the berries are a good food source.
• The male is a persistent singer, vocalizing even through the heat of a summer day. A young male doesn't learn his couplet song from his parents, but from neighboring males during his first year on his own. • Planting coneflowers, cosmos or foxtail grasses may attract Indigo Buntings to your backyard.

Other ID: beady, black eyes; black legs; no wing bars. *Male:* bright blue overall; black lores. *Female:* soft brown overall; whitish throat.
Size: L 5½ in; W 8 in.
Voice: song consists of paired warbled whistles: *fire-fire, where-where, here-here, see-it see-it;* call is a quick *spit.*
Status: abundant migrant and summer resident.
Habitat: deciduous forest and woodland edges, regenerating forest clearings, orchards and shrubby fields.

Similar Birds

Blue Grosbeak (p. 168)

Eastern Bluebird (p. 130)

darker blue head

gray, conical bill

♂

♀

breeding

faint brown streaks on breast

wings and tail may show some black

Nesting: in a small tree, shrub or within a vine tangle; female builds a cup nest of grass, leaves and bark strips; unmarked, white to bluish white eggs are ¾ x ½ in; female incubates 3–4 eggs for 12–13 days.

Did You Know?

Females choose the most melodious males as mates, because these males can usually establish territories with the finest habitat.

Look For

The Indigo Bunting will land midway on a stem of grass or a weed and shuffle slowly toward the seed head, bending down the stem to reach the seeds.

Red-winged Blackbird
Agelaius phoeniceus

The male Red-winged Blackbird wears his bright red shoulders like armor—together with his short, raspy song, they are key in defending his territory from rivals. In field experiments, males whose red shoulders were painted black soon lost their territories. • Nearly every cattail marsh worthy of note in Missouri hosts Red-winged Blackbirds during at least some of the year. • The female's cryptic coloration allows her to sit inconspicuously on her nest, blending in perfectly with the surroundings.

Other ID: *Male:* black overall. *Female:* mottled brown upperparts; pale "eyebrow."
Size: *L* 7½–9 in; *W* 13 in.
Voice: song is a loud, raspy *konk-a-ree* or *ogle-reeeee;* calls include a harsh *check* and high *tseert;* female gives a loud *che-che-che chee chee chee.*
Status: common permanent resident.
Habitat: cattail marshes, wet meadows and ditches, croplands and shoreline shrubs.

Similar Birds

Brewer's Blackbird

Rusty Blackbird

Brown-headed Cowbird (p. 176)

faint, red
shoulder
patch

♂

red shoulder
patch edged
in yellow

heavily streaked
underparts

♀

Nesting: colonial; in cattails or shoreline bushes; female builds an open cup nest of dried cattail leaves lined with fine grass; darkly marked, pale bluish green eggs are 1 x ¾ in; female incubates 3–4 eggs for 10–12 days.

Did You Know?

Some scientists believe that the Red-winged Blackbird is the most abundant bird species in North America.

Look For

As he sings his *konk-a-ree* song, the male Red-winged Blackbird spreads his shoulders to display his bright red epaulets to rivals and potential mates.

Eastern Meadowlark
Sturnella magna

The drab dress of most female songbirds lends them and their nestlings protection during the breeding season, but the female Eastern Meadowlark uses a different strategy. Her V-shaped "necklace" and bright yellow throat and belly create a colorful distraction that leads predators away from the nest. A female flushed from the nest while incubating her eggs will often abandon the nest, and though she will never abandon her chicks, her extra vigilance following a threat usually results in less frequent feeding of nestlings. • Male and female Eastern Meadowlarks look alike.

Other ID: yellow underparts; mottled brown upperparts; long, sharp bill; blackish crown stripes and eye line; pale "eyebrow" and median crown stripe; long, pinkish legs.
Size: L 9–9½ in; W 14 in.
Voice: song is a rich series of 2–8 melodic, clear, slurred whistles: see-*you at school-today* or *this is the year;* gives a rattling flight call and a high, buzzy *dzeart.*
Status: common summer resident; less common in winter.
Habitat: grassy meadows and pastures, some croplands, grassy roadsides and old orchards; also coastal barrens in migration and winter.

Similar Birds

Western Meadowlark

Dickcissel

yellow lores

white jaw line

short, wide tail with white outer tail feathers

broad, black breast band

dark streaking on white sides and flanks

breeding

Nesting: in a concealed depression on the ground; female builds a domed grass nest, woven into surrounding vegetation; heavily spotted, white eggs are 1⅛ x ¾ in; female incubates 3–7 eggs for 13–15 days.

Did You Know?

Although the name suggests that this bird is a lark, it is actually a brightly colored member of the blackbird family.

Look For

The Eastern Meadowlark often whistles its proud song from fence posts and power lines. Song is the best way to tell it apart from the Western Meadowlark.

Brown-headed Cowbird

Molothrus ater

These nomads historically followed bison herds across the Great Plains (they now follow cattle), so they never stayed in one area long enough to build and tend a nest. Instead, cowbirds lay their eggs in other birds' nests, relying on the unsuspecting adoptive parents to incubate the eggs and feed the aggressive young. Orioles, warblers, vireos and tanagers are among the most affected species. Increased livestock farming and fragmentation of forests has encouraged the expansion of the cowbird's range. It is known to parasitize more than 140 bird species.

Other ID: dark eyes; thick, conical bill.
Size: *L* 6–8 in; *W* 12 in.
Voice: song is a high, liquidy gurgle: *glug-ahl-whee* or *bubbloozeee;* call is a squeaky, high-pitched *seep, psee* or *wee-tse-tse* or fast, chipping *ch-ch-ch-ch-ch-ch.*
Status: common permanent resident; less common in winter.
Habitat: agricultural and residential areas, usually fields, woodland edges, roadsides, landfills, campgrounds and areas near cattle.

Similar Birds

Rusty Blackbird

Brewer's Blackbird

Red-winged Blackbird

pale throat

dark brown head

light brown
underparts with
faint streaking

♀

iridescent, green-
blue body plumage
looks glossy black

♂

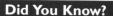

squared tail

Nesting: does not build a nest; female lays up to 40 eggs a year in the nests of other birds, usually 1 egg per nest; brown-speckled, whitish eggs are ⅞ x ⅝ in; eggs hatch after 10–13 days.

Did You Know?

When courting a female, the male cowbird points his bill upward to the sky, fans his tail and wings and utters a loud *squeek*.

Look For

When cowbirds feed in flocks, they hold their back ends up high, with their tails sticking straight up in the air.

Orchard Oriole
Icterus spurius

Orchards may once have been favored haunts of this oriole, but because orchards are now heavily sprayed and manicured, it is unlikely that you will ever see this bird in such a locale. Instead, the Orchard Oriole is most commonly found in large shade trees that line roads, paths and streams. Smaller than all other North American orioles, the Orchard Oriole is one of only two oriole species commonly found in the eastern United States. • These orioles are frequent victims of nest parasitism by Brown-headed Cowbirds. In some parts of its breeding range, over half of Orchard Oriole nests are parasitized by cowbirds.

Other ID: *Male:* black tail. *Female and immature:* olive upperparts; yellow to olive yellow underparts.
Size: L 6–7 in; W 9½ in.
Voice: song is a loud, rapid, varied series of whistled notes; call is a quick *chuck*.
Status: fairly common summer resident.
Habitat: open woodlands, suburban parklands, forest edges, hedgerows and groves of shade trees.

Similar Birds

Baltimore Oriole

Summer Tanager
(p. 156)

Scarlet Tanager

black "hood"

faint white wing bars
on dusky gray wings

♂

♀

dark wings with
white wing bar and
feather edgings

chestnut underparts,
shoulder and rump

Nesting: in the fork of a deciduous tree or
shrub; female builds a hanging pouch nest woven
from grass and plant fibers; sparsely marked, pale
bluish white eggs are ¾ x ⁹⁄₁₆ in; female incubates
4–5 eggs for 12–15 days.

Did You Know?

The Orchard Oriole is
one of the first species to
migrate following breeding
and is usually absent by
the beginning of August.

Look For

Orchard Orioles are best
seen in spring when eager
males hop from branch to
branch, singing their quick,
musical courtship songs.

American Goldfinch
Carduelis tristis

Like vibrant rays of sunshine, American Goldfinches cheerily flutter over weedy fields, gardens and along roadsides. It's hard to miss their jubilant *po-ta-to-chip* call and their distinctive, undulating flight style.
• Because these acrobatic birds regularly feed while hanging upside down, finch feeders have been designed with the seed openings below the perches. These feeders discourage more aggressive House Sparrows, which feed upright, from stealing the seeds. Use niger or black-oil sunflower seeds to attract American Goldfinches to your bird feeder.

Other ID: *Breeding male:* orange bill and legs. *Female:* yellow throat and breast; yellow-green belly. *Nonbreeding male:* olive brown back; yellow-tinged head; gray underparts.
Size: *L* 4½–5 in; *W* 9 in.
Voice: song is a long, varied series of trills, twitters, warbles and hissing notes; calls include *po-ta-to-chip* or *per-chic-or-ee* (often delivered in flight) and a whistled *dear-me, see-me.*
Status: common permanent resident.
Habitat: weedy fields, woodland edges, meadows, riparian areas, parks and gardens.

Similar Birds

Evening Grosbeak

Wilson's Warbler

yellow-green
upperparts

black cap extends
onto forehead

breeding

♀

black wings and
tail with white
wing bars

♂

white rump and
undertail coverts

Nesting: in the fork of a deciduous tree; compact cup nest of plant fibers, grass and spider silk; pale bluish, spotted eggs are ⅝ x ½ in; female incubates 4–6 eggs for 12–14 days.

Did You Know?

These birds nest in late summer to ensure that there is a dependable source of seeds from thistles and dandelions to feed their young.

Look For

American Goldfinches delight in perching on late-summer thistle heads or poking through dandelion patches in search of seeds.

House Sparrow
Passer domesticus

A black "mask" and "bib" adorn the male of this adaptive, aggressive species. The House Sparrow's tendency to usurp territory has led to a decline in native bird populations. This sparrow will even help itself to the convenience of another bird's home, such as a bluebird or Cliff Swallow nest or a Purple Martin house. • This abundant and conspicuous bird was introduced to North America in the 1850s as part of a plan to control the insects that were damaging grain and cereal crops. As it turns out, these birds are primarily vegetarian!

Other ID: *Breeding male:* gray crown; black bill; dark, mottled upperparts; gray underparts; white wing bar. *Female:* indistinct facial patterns; plain gray-brown overall; streaked upperparts.
Size: *L* 5½–6½ in; *W* 9½ in.
Voice: song is a plain, familiar *cheep-cheep-cheep-cheep;* call is a short *chill-up.*
Status: common to locally abundant permanent resident.
Habitat: townsites, urban and suburban areas, farmyards and agricultural areas, railroad yards and other developed areas.

Similar Birds

Harris's Sparrow

House Finch

buffy "eyebrow"

light gray "cheek"

chestnut nape

♀

black lores and "bib"

♂

grayish, unstreaked underparts

breeding

Nesting: often communal; in a birdhouse, ornamental shrub or natural cavity; pair builds a large dome nest of grass, twigs and plant fibers; grayspeckled, white to greenish eggs are ⅞ x ⅝ in; pair incubates 4–6 eggs for 10–13 days.

Did You Know?

A pair of House Sparrows may raise up to four clutches per year, with up to eight young per clutch.

Look For

In spring, House Sparrows feast on the buds of fruit trees. In winter, they flock together in barns in rural areas and at garbage dumps in cities.

Glossary

accipiter: a forest hawk (genus *Accipiter*); characterized by a long tail and short, rounded wings; feeds mostly on birds.

brood: *n.* a family of young from one hatching; *v.* to sit on eggs so as to hatch them.

buteo: a high-soaring hawk (genus *Buteo*); characterized by broad wings and short, wide tails; feeds mostly on small mammals and other land animals.

cere: a fleshy area at the base of a bird's bill that contains the nostrils.

clutch: the number of eggs laid by the female at one time.

corvid: a member of the crow family (Corvidae); includes crows, jays, ravens and magpies.

covey: a group of birds, usually grouse or quail.

crop: an enlargement of the esophagus; serves as a storage structure and (in pigeons) has glands that produce secretions.

dabbling: a foraging technique used by ducks, in which the head and neck are submerged but the body and tail remain on the water's surface; dabbling ducks can usually walk easily on land, can take off without running and have brightly colored speculums.

eclipse plumage: a cryptic plumage, similar to that of females, worn by some male ducks in autumn when they molt their flight feathers and consequently are unable to fly.

fledgling: a young bird that has left the nest but is dependent upon its parents.

flushing: a behavior in which frightened birds explode into flight in response to a disturbance.

flycatching: a feeding behavior in which the bird leaves a perch, snatches an insect in midair and returns to the same perch.

hawking: attempting to catch insects through aerial pursuit.

irruptive: when a bird is abundant in some years and almost absent in others.

leading edge: the front edge of the wing as viewed from below.

mantle: feathers of the back and upperside of folded wings.

morph: one of several alternate plumages displayed by members of a species.

niche: an ecological role filled by a species.

nocturnal: active during the night.

polyandry: a mating strategy in which one female breeds with several males.

precocial: a bird that is relatively well developed at hatching; precocial birds usually have open eyes, extensive down and are fairly mobile.

primaries: the outermost flight feathers.

raptor: a carnivorous (meat-eating) bird; includes eagles, hawks, falcons and owls.

riparian: refers to habitat along riverbanks.

rufous: rusty red in color.

sexual dimorphism: a difference in plumage, size, or other characteristics between males and females of the same species.

speculum: a brightly colored patch on the wings of many dabbling ducks.

stoop: a steep dive through the air, usually performed by birds of prey while foraging or during courtship displays.

Checklist

The following checklist contains 391 species of birds that have been officially recorded in Missouri. Species are grouped by family and listed in taxonomic order in accordance with the A.O.U. *Check-list of North American Birds* (7th ed.) and its supplements.

Accidental and casual species (those that are not seen on a yearly basis) are listed in *italics*. In addition, the following risk categories identified by the Missouri Department of Conservation are also noted: extinct or extirpated (ex), critically imperiled (c), imperiled (im) and vulnerable (v).

Waterfowl
- ❑ *Black-bellied Whistling Duck*
- ❑ *Fulvous Whistling Duck*
- ❑ Greater White-fronted Goose
- ❑ Snow Goose
- ❑ Ross's Goose
- ❑ Cackling Goose
- ❑ Canada Goose
- ❑ *Brant*
- ❑ *Trumpeter Swan*
- ❑ Tundra Swan
- ❑ Wood Duck
- ❑ Gadwall
- ❑ *Eurasian Wigeon*
- ❑ American Wigeon
- ❑ American Black Duck
- ❑ Mallard
- ❑ Blue-winged Teal
- ❑ *Cinnamon Teal*
- ❑ Northern Shoveler
- ❑ Northern Pintail
- ❑ Green-winged Teal
- ❑ Canvasback
- ❑ Redhead
- ❑ Ring-necked Duck
- ❑ Greater Scaup
- ❑ Lesser Scaup
- ❑ *Harlequin Duck*
- ❑ Surf Scoter
- ❑ White-winged Scoter
- ❑ Black Scoter
- ❑ Long-tailed Duck
- ❑ Bufflehead
- ❑ Common Goldeneye
- ❑ *Barrow's Goldeneye*
- ❑ Hooded Merganser
- ❑ Common Merganser
- ❑ Red-breasted Merganser
- ❑ Ruddy Duck

Grouse & Allies
- ❑ *Gray Partridge*
- ❑ Ringed-necked Pheasant
- ❑ Ruffed Grouse
- ❑ Greater Prairie-Chicken (c)
- ❑ Wild Turkey

New World Quails
- ❑ Northern Bobwhite

Loons
- ❑ *Red-throated Loon*
- ❑ *Pacific Loon*
- ❑ Common Loon
- ❑ *Yellow-billed Loon*

Grebes
- ❑ Pied-billed Grebe
- ❑ Horned Grebe
- ❑ *Red-necked Grebe*
- ❑ Eared Grebe
- ❑ Western Grebe
- ❑ *Clark's Grebe*

Storm-Petrels
- ❑ *Band-rumped Storm-Petrel*

Pelicans
- ❑ American White Pelican
- ❑ *Brown Pelican*

Cormorants
- ❑ *Neotropic Cormorant*
- ❑ Double-crested Cormorant

Darters
- ❑ *Anhinga* (ex)

Frigatebirds
- ❑ *Magnificent Frigatebird*

Herons
- ❏ American Bittern (c)
- ❏ Least Bittern (v)
- ❏ Great Blue Heron
- ❏ Great Egret (v)
- ❏ Snowy Egret (c)
- ❏ Little Blue Heron (v)
- ❏ *Tricolored Heron*
- ❏ Cattle Egret
- ❏ Green Heron
- ❏ Black-crowned Night-Heron (v)
- ❏ Yellow-crowned Night-Heron

Ibises
- ❏ White Ibis
- ❏ Glossy Ibis
- ❏ White-face Ibis
- ❏ *Roseate Spoonbill*

Storks
- ❏ *Wood Stork*

Vultures
- ❏ Black Vulture (v)
- ❏ Turkey Vulture

Kites, Hawks & Eagles
- ❏ Osprey
- ❏ *Swallow-tailed Kite* (ex)
- ❏ Mississippi Kite (v)
- ❏ Bald Eagle (c)
- ❏ Northern Harrier (im)
- ❏ Sharp-shinned Hawk (v)
- ❏ Cooper's Hawk
- ❏ Northern Goshawk
- ❏ Red-shouldered Hawk
- ❏ Broad-winged Hawk
- ❏ Swainson's Hawk (im)
- ❏ Red-tailed Hawk
- ❏ *Ferruginous Hawk*
- ❏ Rough-legged Hawk
- ❏ Golden Eagle

Falcons
- ❏ American Kestrel
- ❏ Merlin
- ❏ *Gyrfalcon*
- ❏ Peregrine Falcon (c)
- ❏ Prairie Falcon

Rails, Gallinules & Coots
- ❏ Yellow Rail
- ❏ *Black Rail* (c)
- ❏ King Rail (c)
- ❏ Virginia Rail (im)
- ❏ Sora (im)
- ❏ Purple Gallinule

- ❏ Common Moorhen (im)
- ❏ American Coot

Cranes
- ❏ Sandhill Crane
- ❏ *Whooping Crane*

Plovers
- ❏ Black-bellied Plover
- ❏ American Golden-Plover
- ❏ Snowy Plover
- ❏ Semipalmated Plover
- ❏ Piping Plover
- ❏ Killdeer

Stilts & Avocets
- ❏ Black-necked Stilt
- ❏ American Avocet

Sandpipers & Allies
- ❏ Greater Yellowlegs
- ❏ Lesser Yellowlegs
- ❏ Solitary Sandpiper
- ❏ Willet
- ❏ Spotted Sandpiper
- ❏ Upland Sandpiper
- ❏ *Eskimo Curlew* (ex)
- ❏ Whimbrel
- ❏ *Long-billed Curlew*
- ❏ Hudsonian Godwit
- ❏ Marbled Godwit
- ❏ Ruddy Turnstone
- ❏ Red Knot
- ❏ Sanderling
- ❏ Semipalmated Sandpiper
- ❏ Western Sandpiper
- ❏ *Rufous-necked Stint*
- ❏ Least Sandpiper
- ❏ White-rumped Sandpiper
- ❏ Baird's Sandpiper
- ❏ Pectoral Sandpiper
- ❏ Dunlin
- ❏ Stilt Sandpiper
- ❏ Buff-breasted Sandpiper
- ❏ *Ruff*
- ❏ Short-billed Dowitcher
- ❏ Long-billed Dowitcher
- ❏ Wilson's Snipe
- ❏ American Woodcock
- ❏ Wilson's Phalarope
- ❏ Red-necked Phalarope
- ❏ *Red Phalarope*

Gulls & Allies
- ❏ *Pomarine Jaeger*
- ❏ *Parasitic Jaeger*
- ❏ *Long-tailed Jaeger*

- ❏ *Laughing Gull*
- ❏ *Franklin's Gull*
- ❏ *Little Gull*
- ❏ *Black-headed Gull*
- ❏ Bonaparte's Gull
- ❏ *Mew Gull*
- ❏ Ring-billed Gull
- ❏ *California Gull*
- ❏ Herring Gull
- ❏ *Thayer's Gull*
- ❏ *Iceland Gull*
- ❏ *Lesser Black-backed Gull*
- ❏ *Slaty-backed Gull*
- ❏ Glaucous Gull
- ❏ *Great Black-backed Gull*
- ❏ *Sabine's Gull*
- ❏ Black-legged Kittiwake
- ❏ Caspian Tern
- ❏ Common Tern
- ❏ Forster's Tern
- ❏ Least Tern (c)
- ❏ Black Tern

Pigeons & Doves
- ❏ Rock Pigeon
- ❏ *Band-tailed Pigeon*
- ❏ Eurasian Collared-Dove
- ❏ *White-winged Dove*
- ❏ Mourning Dove
- ❏ *Passenger Pigeon* (ex)
- ❏ *Inca Dove*
- ❏ *Common Ground-Dove*

Parrots
- ❏ *Carolina Parakeet* (ex)

Cuckoos
- ❏ Black-billed Cuckoo
- ❏ Yellow-billed Cuckoo
- ❏ Greater Roadrunner (v)

Anis
- ❏ *Groove-billed Ani*

Barn Owls
- ❏ Barn Owl (v)

Owls
- ❏ Eastern Screech-Owl
- ❏ Great Horned Owl
- ❏ Snowy Owl
- ❏ *Burrowing Owl*
- ❏ Barred Owl
- ❏ Long-eared Owl
- ❏ Short-eared Owl (im)
- ❏ Northern Saw-whet Owl

Nightjars
- ❏ Common Nighthawk
- ❏ Chuck-will's-widow
- ❏ Whip-poor-will

Swifts
- ❏ Chimney Swift
- ❏ *White-throated Swift*

Hummingbirds
- ❏ Ruby-throated Hummingbird
- ❏ *Rufous Hummingbird*

Kingfishers
- ❏ Belted Kingfisher

Woodpeckers
- ❏ *Lewis's Woodpecker*
- ❏ Red-headed Woodpecker
- ❏ Red-bellied Woodpecker
- ❏ Yellow-bellied Sapsucker
- ❏ Downy Woodpecker
- ❏ Hairy Woodpecker
- ❏ *Red-cockaded Woodpecker* (ex)
- ❏ Northern Flicker
- ❏ Pileated Woodpecker
- ❏ *Ivory-billed Woodpecker* (ex)

Flycatchers
- ❏ Olive-sided Flycatcher
- ❏ Eastern Wood-Pewee
- ❏ Yellow-bellied Flycatcher
- ❏ Acadian Flycatcher
- ❏ Alder Flycatcher
- ❏ Willow Flycatcher
- ❏ Least Flycatcher
- ❏ Eastern Phoebe
- ❏ *Say's Phoebe*
- ❏ *Vermilion Flycatcher*
- ❏ Great Crested Flycatcher
- ❏ Western Kingbird
- ❏ Eastern Kingbird
- ❏ Scissor-tailed Flycatcher

Shrikes
- ❏ Loggerhead Shrike (im)
- ❏ Northern Shrike

Vireos
- ❏ White-eyed Vireo
- ❏ Bell's Vireo
- ❏ Yellow-throated Vireo
- ❏ Blue-headed Vireo
- ❏ Warbling Vireo
- ❏ Philadelphia Vireo
- ❏ Red-eyed Vireo

Jays & Crows
- ❑ Blue Jay
- ❑ *Clark's Nutcracker*
- ❑ *Black-billed Magpie*
- ❑ American Crow
- ❑ Fish Crow
- ❑ *Common Raven* (ex)

Larks
- ❑ Horned Lark

Swallows
- ❑ Purple Martin
- ❑ Tree Swallow
- ❑ Northern Rough-winged Swallow
- ❑ Bank Swallow
- ❑ Cliff Swallow
- ❑ Barn Swallow

Chickadees & Titmice
- ❑ Carolina Chickadee
- ❑ Black-capped Chickadee
- ❑ Tufted Titmouse

Nuthatches
- ❑ Red-breasted Nuthatch
- ❑ White-breasted Nuthatch
- ❑ *Brown-headed Nuthatch* (ex)

Creepers
- ❑ Brown Creeper

Wrens
- ❑ *Rock Wren*
- ❑ Carolina Wren
- ❑ Bewick's Wren
- ❑ House Wren
- ❑ Winter Wren
- ❑ Sedge Wren
- ❑ Marsh Wren (v)

Kinglets
- ❑ Golden-crowned Kinglet
- ❑ Ruby-crowned Kinglet

Gnatcatchers
- ❑ Blue-gray Gnatcatcher

Thrushes
- ❑ Eastern Bluebird
- ❑ *Mountain Bluebird*
- ❑ Townsend's Solitaire
- ❑ Veery
- ❑ Gray-cheeked Thrush
- ❑ Swainson's Thrush
- ❑ Hermit Thrush
- ❑ Wood Thrush
- ❑ American Robin
- ❑ *Varied Thrush*

Mockingbirds & Thrashers
- ❑ Gray Catbird
- ❑ Northern Mockingbird
- ❑ *Sage Thrasher*
- ❑ Brown Thrasher

Starlings
- ❑ European Starling

Wagtails & Pipits
- ❑ American Pipit
- ❑ Sprague's Pipit

Waxwings
- ❑ *Bohemian Waxwing*
- ❑ Cedar Waxwing

Wood-Warblers
- ❑ *Bachman's Warbler* (ex)
- ❑ Blue-winged Warbler
- ❑ Golden-winged Warbler
- ❑ Tennessee Warbler
- ❑ Orange-crowned Warbler
- ❑ Nashville Warbler
- ❑ Northern Parula
- ❑ Yellow Warbler
- ❑ Chestnut-sided Warbler (v)
- ❑ Magnolia Warbler
- ❑ Cape May Warbler
- ❑ Black-throated Blue Warbler
- ❑ Yellow-rumped Warbler
- ❑ Black-throated Green Warbler
- ❑ *Hermit Warbler*
- ❑ Blackburnian Warbler
- ❑ Yellow-throated Warbler
- ❑ Pine Warbler
- ❑ Prairie Warbler
- ❑ Palm Warbler
- ❑ Bay-breasted Warbler
- ❑ Blackpoll Warbler
- ❑ Cerulean Warbler (v)
- ❑ Black-and-white Warbler
- ❑ American Redstart
- ❑ Prothonotary Warbler
- ❑ Worm-eating Warbler
- ❑ Swainson's Warbler (im)
- ❑ Ovenbird
- ❑ Northern Waterthrush
- ❑ Louisiana Waterthrush
- ❑ Kentucky Warbler
- ❑ Connecticut Warbler
- ❑ Mourning Warbler
- ❑ *MacGillivray's Warbler*
- ❑ Common Yellowthroat

❏ Hooded Warbler (v)
❏ Wilson's Warbler
❏ Canada Warbler
❏ Yellow-breasted Chat

Tanagers
❏ Summer Tanager
❏ Scarlet Tanager
❏ *Western Tanager*

Sparrows & Allies
❏ *Green-tailed Towhee*
❏ Spotted Towhee
❏ Eastern Towhee
❏ Bachman's Sparrow (im)
❏ American Tree Sparrow
❏ Chipping Sparrow
❏ Clay-colored Sparrow
❏ Field Sparrow
❏ Vesper Sparrow
❏ Lark Sparrow
❏ *Lark Bunting*
❏ Savannah Sparrow
❏ Grasshopper Sparrow
❏ Henslow's Sparrow (sc)
❏ Le Conte's Sparrow
❏ Nelson's Sharp-tailed Sparrow
❏ Fox Sparrow
❏ Song Sparrow
❏ Lincoln's Sparrow
❏ Swamp Sparrow
❏ White-throated Sparrow
❏ Harris's Sparrow
❏ White-crowned Sparrow
❏ Dark-eyed Junco
❏ *McCown's Longspur*
❏ Lapland Longspur
❏ Smith's Longspur
❏ *Chestnut-collared Longspur*
❏ Snow Bunting

Grosbeaks & Buntings
❏ Northern Cardinal
❏ Rose-breasted Grosbeak
❏ Black-headed Grosbeak
❏ Blue Grosbeak
❏ *Lazuli Bunting*
❏ Indigo Bunting
❏ Painted Bunting (v)
❏ Dickcissel

Blackbirds & Allies
❏ Bobolink
❏ Red-winged Blackbird
❏ Eastern Meadowlark
❏ Western Meadowlark
❏ Yellow-headed Blackbird (v)
❏ Rusty Blackbird
❏ Brewer's Blackbird
❏ Common Grackle
❏ Great-tailed Grackle
❏ *Bronzed Cowbird*
❏ Brown-headed Cowbird
❏ Orchard Oriole
❏ Baltimore Oriole

Finches
❏ *Pine Grosbeak*
❏ Purple Finch
❏ House Finch
❏ Red Crossbill
❏ White-winged Crossbill
❏ Common Redpoll
❏ Pine Siskin
❏ *Lesser Goldfinch*
❏ American Goldfinch
❏ Evening Grosbeak

Old World Sparrows
❏ House Sparrow
❏ Eurasian Tree Sparrow

Sources

Audubon Society of Missouri. "Annotated Checklist of Missouri Birds." http://mobirds.org/MBRC/MOChecklist.asp (accessed December 15, 2005).

Missouri Department of Conservation. "Seasonal List of the Standard Birds of Missouri." http://mdc.mo.gov/nathis/birds/emobirds/seasonal.htm (December 15, 2005).

Missouri Department of Conservation. "Missouri Species and Communities of Conservation Concern." http://mdc.mo.gov/documents/nathis/endangered/checklist.pdf (accessed January 5, 2006).

Robbins, Mark B. and David A. Easterla. 1992. *Birds of Missouri: Their Distribution and Abundance.* University of Missouri Press, Columbia, MO.

USGS Northern Prairie Wildlife Research Center. "Bird Checklists of the United States: Missouri." http://www.npwrc.usgs.gov/resource/othrdata/chekbird/r3/29.htm (accessed December 17, 2005).

Index